Peter Roe Series XXV

Númenor, the Mighty and Frail

Proceedings of The Tolkien Society
Seminar 2023

Edited by Will Sherwood

Copyright © 2025 by The Tolkien Society
www.tolkiensociety.org

First published 2025 by Luna Press Publishing, Edinburgh
www.lunapresspublishing.com

ISBN-13: 978-1-915556-16-5

Cover illustration 'Argonath of Gondor' © Kip Rasmussen 2022

All contributors to this volume assert their moral right to be identified as the author of their individual contributions.

Each contribution remains the intellectual property of its respective author and is published by The Tolkien Society, an educational charity (number 273809) registered in England and Wales, under a non-exclusive licence.

All rights reserved by The Tolkien Society. No part of this publication may be reproduced, stored in a retrieval system, or transmitted in any form or by any means, electronic, mechanical, photocopy, recording or otherwise, without prior written permission of the copyright holder. Nor can it be circulated in any form of binding or cover other than that in which it is published and without similar condition including this condition being imposed on a subsequent purchaser.

Contents

About the Peter Roe Memorial Fund v
The Peter Roe Series vii
Abbreviations ix

Introduction
Will Sherwood 1

Sea Goddess Worship and the Power of the King: Parallel between Aldarion, Uinen, Mataram Sultanate, and Javanese Queen of the Southern Sea
Putri Prihatini 10

Penguasa Laut dan Sang Raja: Paralel antara Aldarion, Uinen, Kesultanan Mataram, dan Ratu Laut Selatan Jawa
Putri Prihatini 22

Dealing with the Dead: Nuances of ancient Egypt and medieval theology in Númenor
Irina Metzler 35

"I often dream of it": Trauma and memory in the legacy of the Downfall of Númenor
S.R. Westvik 52

"Foretasting Death in Life": Desire, the Fall, and Attempting to Return the 'Gift' of Ilúvatar
Sara Brown 72

"All roads are now bent": Ethical Readings of the Corporeality of Númenor
Journee Cotton 88

Ecology of Imperialism: Environmental History for Númenor
Muhammed Alpaslan Tandırcı 98

The 'Akallabêth' and the Anthropocene: Myth, Ecology, and the Changing of the World
Erik Jampa Andersson 109

Monstrous (Im)mortality: Transhumanism and Ecocriticism in 'Akallabêth'
Kristine Larsen 130

"By the Waters of Anduin We Lay Down and Wept": Exilic Theology in the 'Akallabêth'
Rev. Tom Emanuel 148

Seducer-Destroyer: Sauron's Femme Fatale Sources and their Role in the Númenor Narrative
Mercury Natis 160

Elmar, the Experience of Captured Women, and Empires in Decline
Clare Moore 178

About the contributors 189

About the Peter Roe Memorial Fund

The Tolkien Society's seminar proceedings and other booklets are typically published under the auspices of the Peter Roe Memorial Fund, a fund in the Society's accounts that commemorates a young member who died in a traffic accident. Peter Roe, a young and very talented person joined the Society in 1979, shortly after his sixteenth birthday. He had discovered Middle-earth some time earlier, and was so inspired by it that he even developed his own system of runes, similar to the Dwarvish Angerthas, but which utilised logical sound values, matching the logical shapes of the runes. Peter was also an accomplished cartographer, and his bedroom was covered with multi-coloured maps of the journeys of the fellowship, plans of Middle-earth, and other drawings.

Peter was also a creative writer in both poetry and prose—the subject being incorporated into his own *Dwarvish Chronicles*. He was so enthusiastic about having joined the Society that he had written a letter ordering all the available back issues, and was on his way to buy envelopes when he was hit by a speeding lorry outside his home.

Sometime later, Jonathan and Lester Simons (at that time Chairman and Membership Secretary respectively) visited Peter's parents to see his room and to look at the work on which he had spent so much care and attention in such a tragically short life. It was obvious that Peter had produced, and would have continued to produce, material of such a high standard as to make a complete booklet, with poetry, calligraphy, stories and cartography. The then committee set up a special account in honour of Peter, with the consent of his parents, which would be the source of finance for the Society's special publications. Over the years a number of members have made generous donations to the fund.

The first publication to be financed by the Peter Roe Memorial Fund was *Some Light on Middle-earth* by Edward Crawford, published in 1985. Subsequent publications have been composed from papers delivered at Tolkien Society workshops and seminars, talks from guest speakers at the Annual Dinner, and collections of the best articles from past issues of *Amon Hen*, the Society's bulletin.

Dwarvish Fragments, an unfinished tale by Peter, was printed in *Mallorn* 15 (September 1980). A standalone collection of Peter's creative endeavours is currently being prepared for publication.

The Peter Roe Series

I	*Some Light on Middle-earth*, ed. by Edward Crawford (Pinner: The Tolkien Society, 1985)
II	*Leaves from the Tree: Tolkien's Short Fiction*, ed. by Trevor Reynolds (London: The Tolkien Society, 1991)
III	*The First and Second Ages*, ed. by Trevor Reynolds (London: The Tolkien Society, 1992; Edinburgh: Luna Press Publishing, 2020)
IV	*Travel and Communication in Tolkien's Worlds*, ed. by Richard Crawshaw (Swindon: The Tolkien Society, 1996)
V	*Digging Potatoes, Growing Trees: Volume One*, ed. by Helen Armstrong (Swindon: The Tolkien Society, 1997)
VI	*Digging Potatoes, Growing Trees: Volume Two*, ed. by Helen Armstrong (Telford: The Tolkien Society, 1998)
VII	*Tolkien, the Sea and Scandinavia*, ed. by Richard Crawshaw (Telford: The Tolkien Society, 1999; Edinburgh: Luna Press Publishing, 2021)
VIII	*The Ways of Creative Mythologies*, ed. by Maria Kuteeva, 2 vols (Telford: The Tolkien Society, 2000)
IX	*Tolkien: A Mythology for England?*, ed. by Richard Crawshaw (Telford: The Tolkien Society, 2000)
X	*The Best of Amon Hen: Part One*, ed. by Andrew Wells, (Telford: The Tolkien Society, 2000)
XI	*Digging Potatoes, Growing Trees: Volume Three*, ed. by Helen Armstrong (Telford: The Tolkien Society, 2001)
XII	*Sindarin Lexicon*, Kenneth Chaij (Telford: The Tolkien Society, 2001)

XIII	*The Best of Amon Hen: Part Two*, ed. by Andrew Wells (Telford: The Tolkien Society, 2002)
XIV	*Tolkien: Influenced and Influencing*, ed. by Matthew Vernon (Telford: The Tolkien Society, 2005)
XV	*Freedom, Fate and Choice in Middle-earth*, ed. by Christopher Kreuzer (London: The Tolkien Society, 2012)
XVI	*Journeys & Destinations*, ed. by Ian Collier (Wolverhampton: The Tolkien Society, 2015)
XVII	*Death and Immortality in Middle-earth*, ed. by Daniel Helen (Edinburgh: Luna Press Publishing, 2017)
XVIII	*Poetry and Song in the works of J.R.R. Tolkien*, ed. by Anna Milon (Edinburgh: Luna Press Publishing, 2018)
XIX	*Tolkien the Pagan? Reading Middle-earth through a spiritual lens*, ed. by Anna Milon (Edinburgh: Luna Press Publishing, 2019).
XX	*Adapting Tolkien*, ed. by Will Sherwood (Ediburgh: Luna Press Publishing, 2021)
XXI	*Twenty-First Century Receptions of Tolkien*, ed. by Will Sherwood (Edinburgh: Luna Press Publishing, 2022)
XXII	*Tolkien and Diversity*, ed. by Will Sherwood (Edinburgh: Luna Press Publising 2023)
XXIII	*Translating and Illustrating Tolkien*, ed. by Will Sherwood (Edinburgh: Luna Press Publishing 2023)
XXIV	*Tolkien and the Gothic*, ed. by Will Sherwood (Edinburgh: Luna Press Publishing 2024)
XXV	*Númenor, the Mighty and Frail*, ed. by Will Sherwood (Edinburgh: Luna Press Publishing 2025)

Abbreviations

A&I	*The Lay of Aotrou and Itroun*, ed. by Verlyn Flieger (London: HarperCollins, 2016)
Arthur	*The Fall of Arthur,* ed. by Christopher Tolkien (London: HarperCollins, 2013; Boston: Houghton Mifflin Harcourt, 2013)
AW	*Ancrene Wisse* (Oxford: Oxford University Press, 1962)
B&L	*Beren and Lúthien*, ed. by Christopher Tolkien (London: HarperCollins, 2017)
Beowulf	*Beowulf: A Translation and Commentary, together with Sellic Spell*, ed. by Christopher Tolkien (London: HarperCollins, 2014; Boston: Houghton Mifflin Harcourt, 2014)
Bombadil	*The Adventures of Tom Bombadil and other verses from the Red Book* (London: George Allen & Unwin, 1962; Boston: Houghton Mifflin, 1962)
CoH	*The Children of Húrin*, ed. by Christopher Tolkien (London: HarperCollins, 2007; Boston: Houghton Mifflin Harcourt, 2007)
Exodus	*The Old English Exodus*, ed. by Joan Turville-Petre (Oxford: Oxford University Press, 1982)
Father Christmas	*Letters from Father Christmas*, ed. by Baillie Tolkien (London: George Allen & Unwin, 1976; Boston: Houghton Mifflin, 1976)

FoG	*The Fall of Gondolin*, ed. by Christopher Tolkien (London: HarperCollins, 2018).
FoN	*The Fall of Númenor and Other Tales from the Second Age of Middle-earth*, ed. Brian Sibley (London: Harper Collins, 2022).
FR	*The Fellowship of the Ring*
Hobbit	*The Hobbit*
Jewels	*The War of the Jewels,* ed. by Christopher Tolkien (London: HarperCollins, 1994; Boston: Houghton Mifflin, 1994)
Kullervo	*The Story of Kullervo,* ed. by Verlyn Flieger (London: HarperCollins, 2015; Boston: Houghton Mifflin Harcourt, 2016)
Lays	*The Lays of Beleriand,* ed. by Christopher Tolkien (London: George Allen & Unwin, 1985; Boston: Houghton Mifflin, 1985)
Letters	*The Letters of J.R.R. Tolkien,* ed. by Humphrey Carpenter with the assistance of Christopher Tolkien (London: George Allen & Unwin, 1981; Boston: Houghton Mifflin, 1981)
Lost Road	*The Lost Road and Other Writings*, ed. by Christopher Tolkien (London: Unwin Hyman, 1987; Boston: Houghton Mifflin, 1987)
Lost Tales I	*The Book of Lost Tales, Part One,* ed. by Christopher Tolkien (London: George Allen & Unwin, 1983; Boston: Houghton Mifflin, 1984)

Lost Tales II	*The Book of Lost Tales, Part Two*, ed. by Christopher Tolkien (London: George Allen & Unwin, 1984; Boston: Houghton Mifflin, 1984)
Monsters	*The Monsters and the Critics and Other Essays* (London: George Allen & Unwin, 1983; Boston: Houghton Mifflin, 1984)
Morgoth	*Morgoth's Ring*, ed. by Christopher Tolkien (London: Geore, 1993; Boston: Houghton Mifflin, 1993)
OFS	*Tolkien On Fairy-stories*, ed. by Verlyn Flieger and Douglas A. Anderson (London: HarperCollins, 2008)
P&S	*Poems and Stories* (London: George Allen & Unwin, 1980; Boston: Houghton Mifflin, 1994)
Peoples	*The Peoples of Middle-earth*, ed. by Christopher Tolkien (London: HarperCollins, 1996; Boston: Houghton Mifflin, 1996)
Perilous Realm	*Tales from the Perilous Realm* (London: HarperCollins, 1997)
RK	*The Return of the King*
Silmarillion	*The Silmarillion*, ed. by Christopher Tolkien (London: George Allen & Unwin, 1977; Boston: Houghton Mifflin, 1977).
Sauron	*Sauron Defeated*, ed. by Christopher Tolkien (London: HarperCollins, 1992; Boston: Houghton Mifflin, 1992)

Secret Vice	*A Secret Vice: Tolkien on Invented Languages*, ed. by Dimitra Fimi and Andrew Higgins (London: HarperCollins, 2016)
Shadow	*The Return of the Shadow*, ed. by Christopher Tolkien (London: Unwin Hyman, 1988; Boston: Houghton Mifflin, 1988)
Shaping	*The Shaping of Middle-earth*, ed. by Christopher Tolkien (London: George Allen & Unwin, 1986; Boston: Houghton Mifflin, 1986)
S&G	*The Legend of Sigurd and Gudrún*, ed. by Christopher Tolkien (London: HarperCollins, 2009; Boston: Houghton Mifflin Harcourt, 2009)
TL	*Tree and Leaf*, 2nd edn (London: Unwin Hyman, 1988; Boston: Houghton Mifflin, 1989)
TT	*The Two Towers*
Treason	*The Treason of Isengard*, ed. by Christopher Tolkien (London: Unwin Hyman; Boston: Houghton Mifflin, 1989)
UT	*Unfinished Tales of Númenor and Middle-earth*, ed. by Christopher Tolkien (London: George Allen & Unwin, 1980; Boston: Houghton Mifflin, 1980)
War	*The War of the Ring*, ed. by Christopher Tolkien (London: Unwin Hyman, 1990; Boston: Houghton Mifflin, 1990)

Introduction

Will Sherwood

Númenor holds a unique place in the evolution of J.R.R. Tolkien's writing. Not only did the island come to occupy a central space within the Second and Third Ages of Arda, it also informed multiple time-travel narratives affiliated to varying degrees with his legendarium. In *The Lost Road and Other Writings* (1987), Christopher Tolkien confidently asserts that "Númenor […] arose in the actual context of [Tolkien's] discussion with C. S. Lewis in […] 1936" (9). There "never was a time when the legends of Númenor were 'unrelated to the main mythology'" and after Tolkien abandoned 'The Lost Road' (10), Númenor became fully integrated into the legendarium, "thus inaugurating the Second Age" and setting the stage for Aragorn II's ascension to the throne of Gondor as the heir of Elendil (8).

Indeed, the story of Númenor's downfall, the long histories of Arnor and Gondor, and the gradual fading of the Dúnedain are more fully realised in *The Lord of the Rings* (1954-1955) in tandem with Aragorn's development in the Rivendell chapters and Faramir's conversation with the Hobbits at Henneth Annûn. While this may indicate that Númenor and the Númenóreans, an island and people in turn romanticised and shrouded in nostalgia and pain, became a crucial part of Middle-earth's "vast backcloths" through the composition of *The Lord of the*

Rings, it also stands as a critical hinge between the passing of the mythical First Age and the more historically minded Second and Third Ages (*Letters*, Letter 131, 203). This transition in the late 1930s, what Dimitra Fimi terms the "historical continuation" of the legendarium (2009, 117), paved the way for Tolkien's oft-quoted declaration "I much prefer history, true or feigned" in the 'Foreword to the Second Edition' of *The Lord of the Rings* (xx). Although Númenor maintains a prolific position within the legendarium (given its legacies in the Third and Fourth Ages), its creation and inclusion prompted a significant shift in how Tolkien conceived of and wrote about Middle-earth.

Tolkien's penchant for framed narratives is well known. From Eriol's and Ælfwine's inclusion as mediators of the Fairies'/Elves' myths, history, and culture in *The Book of Lost Tales* to the The Red Book of Westmarch being written by the Hobbits, Tolkien was consistently conscious of *how* history was being constructed, and, perhaps more importantly, *whose* hand was forging said history. Elendil takes a central role in ensuring that the history of Númenor is preserved in Middle-earth. Tolkien states in 'The Line of Elros: Kings of Númenor' that the "deeds of Ar-Pharazôn [...] is told in the tale of the Downfall of Númenor, *which Elendil wrote*, and which was preserved in Gondor" (*UT*, 224; emphasis mine). In his notes, Christopher elaborates that 'Aldarion and Erendis: The Mariner's Wife' is "one of the few detailed histories preserved from Númenor" and that it owes its "preservation" to Elendil (227).

Elendil's political status as one of the Faithful and the trauma inflicted from the downfall of Númenor therefore raises questions over his authorial positionality, intent, and his framing of the *dramatis personae* in his writings. This in turn prompts further questions into how Númenor and the Númenóreans are remembered and romanticised by their descendants towards the end of the Third Age. It is worthy of note, for example, that while the original Red Book was not "preserved" (*FR*, 'Prologue', 14), the Thain's Book, the "first" and "most important copy" is "correct[ed]" and edited in Gondor (15). The degrees to which this happens is not recorded, but the editorial practice and interpolations accounted for in 'Note on the Shire Records' ('Prologue') at the beginning of *The Lord of the Rings* does direct us to reconsider the ethics of editing. Before we start to read the tale proper set out in *The Lord of the Rings*, then, Tolkien is explicitly telling us that the history of Middle-earth contained within the novel has been adapted and altered by the hands of Númenor's distant descendants under the request of Aragorn.

Númenor's long legacy thus stretches far into the Fourth Age as is apparent in Gondor's written history, songs, and tales, but it is also observable in the natural world of and divisions of people in Middle-earth. Númenor's mass deforestation of what I have elsewhere termed Tolkien's "primordial arboreal network" has severely scarred the land (2025). Along with Sauron's war on the Elves in the Second Age, the Númenóreans have inflicted an ecological trauma that haunts the Hobbits' travels through the "lonely and unpleasant" (*FR*, 'A Knife in the Dark', 182), "cheerless" and "gloomy" (*FR*, 'Flight to the Ford', 199), "threatening and unfriendly" and "ominous" (201) lands of Eriador towards Rivendell. Even as the Fellowship march south, Eriador remains "bleak" and "dangerous" (*FR*, 'The Ring Goes South', 282), filled with a "dead silence" (284). The Númenóreans are thus partially responsible for the ecocide of the north-west of Middle-earth. Yet on the flipside they also played a crucial part in introducing the mallorn tree to Middle-earth, passing seeds to Gil-galad, who in turn gifts them to Galadriel as she leaves for Lothlórien. However, their engagement with and subjugation of the peoples who already inhabited the regions that would become Arnor and Gondor poses questions into the ethics of the Númenóreans' behaviour towards the Other. Still, they also play a central role in resisting and finally defeating Sauron at the end of the Second Age. And that is before recalling Gondor's extensive struggle against Mordor in the Third Age. But it is also the Númenóreans who triggered the cataclysmic removal of Valinor from Arda. Númenor's legacy is thus thorny, knotted, and complex. At each turn its might and power shines while its ethical and spiritual frailty casts a long shadow on the past, present, and future of Arda's peoples and environments.

While this introduction has provided an overview and comment on multiple important factors of Númenor's place inside and outside the legendarium, there is much that has either been alluded to or not covered due to space. Neither can a single volume cover everything. What the follow proceedings does do is shed light on some parts of Númenor, the Númenóreans, and its/their legacies in Middle-earth. It hopes that by drawing attention to Númenor as a nexus of critical study, it will encourage deeper scholarship on the island and its people.

Númenor, the Mighty and Frail was the Tolkien Society's hybrid seminar of 2023 that took place on Sunday 2nd July in Leeds. It offered in-person and online papers and continued to welcome speakers from across the globe. Proceedings from each seminar are entirely dependent on how many speakers wish to publish their papers afterwards – this directly impacts how much is included in each volume. Speakers are invited to edit and expand their original paper (necessarily restricted by the 20-minute delivery window) to allow sufficient space for their argument and discussion. These points mean that how much of the seminar is represented and the length of each paper and volume constantly varies. Additionally, as the seminar's hybrid function means that the programme needs to accommodate the time zones of online speakers, the ordering of papers in proceedings may differ depending on structural flow and the editor. For the present proceedings, while two of the thirteen authors chose not to publish their papers in this volume, the remaining eleven papers follow the same structure as the seminar. Since *Tolkien and Diversity* (2023), authors in seminar proceedings have been invited to publish their papers in English and their home language. This was implemented to ensure that authors can choose to contribute to and advance Tolkien scholarship in their home language and academy.

Putri Prihatini opens this volume by exploring the parallels between Aldarion's exploits, his connection to the Uinen figure, and how the myth of Kanjeng Ratu Kidul, the Javanese marine goddess known as the "Queen of the Southern Sea", contributed to the power legitimation behind the kingship of Mataram Sultanate.

Irina Metzler follows by examining the two contrasting approaches to the bodies of the dead in Egypt and the Middle Ages, comparing them with the diverse strands of necrological narratives in Tolkien's description of Númenor and Gondor.

Next, S.R. Westvik considers how Númenor and its descendants experienced the traumatic events of the downfall and how this cataclysm was remembered through to the Third Age. Drawing on DSM-5 criteria for diagnosing trauma and PTSD as well as qualitative depictions of trauma, Westvik comments on the place of material and immaterial sources, from memoir to memory, to help illuminate individual and collective approaches to understanding and managing trauma in Tolkien's writings.

Sara Brown proceeds by drawing attention to the moral judgement of Tolkien and Eru Ilúvatar over the Númenóreans' desire for power and possessions which directly informed their acts of colonialism, slavery, and the seizure of natural resources for personal enrichment, addressing the question of whether it is hubris, desire, or fear that is the main catalyst in the fall of Númenor.

Journee Cotton then employs an interdisciplinary framework of health geography and environmental bioethics to argue that there is an embedded connection between the Númenóreans' lust for corporeal immortality and the death and destruction to the bodies of people and Middle-earth. Interlinking the presence of frailty and impacted locations allows Cotton to consider the relationship between geography from a holistic perspective on health, thus demonstrating the connection between the failure of ethics and the detriment of the body of land, and consequently its inhabitants.

Muhammed Alpaslan Tandırcı moves on to read the ecology of imperialism in 'Aldarion and Erendis: The Mariner's Wife', arguing that the Númenóreans' abuse of Middle-earth's natural world and their alienation from Númenor's own directly led to the island's downfall.

Next, Erik Jampa Andersson evaluates how the 'Akallabêth' can help us think critically about the ecological and political dynamics of the 'Anthropocene', offering a critical analysis of the role of the Númenóreans in the narrativization (and potential distortion) of their own 'history', and how their colonial legacy is negotiated both 'in-universe' within the Third Age, and in primary-world adaptations of Tolkien's work.

Kristine Larsen follows by exploring a close transhumanist and ecocritical reading of the 'Akallabêth', considering how through their rejection of their mortal nature they succumb to a vain transhumanist lust for physical immortality, embracing ungodly alchemical experiments.

The Rev. Tom Emanuel turns our attention to how Elendil's grappling with theodicy in the wake of Númenor's downfall mirrors the grappling of exilic and post-exilic biblical prophets such as Jeremiah with theodicy in the wake of the destruction of the Jerusalem Temple and the conquest of the Holy Land.

The penultimate paper by Mercury Natis examines the potential influences for Sauron's character on Númenor, such as Salomé and Lilith, and how this depiction is part of a greater conversation on Sauron's queer presence within the legendarium. It is through the inherent queerness of Sauron, Natis argues, that Tolkien explores the morality of seduction, rather than engaging directly with the sexuality inherent in the concept of the devious temptress.

Clare Moore concludes these proceedings by drawing on contemporary research to provide a comparative reading of 'Tar-Elmar' with Rosemary Sutcliff's *The Lantern Bearers*, examining how both texts imagine what happened to Romano-British women during Anglo-Saxon raids in the fifth century.

On behalf of the Tolkien Society, I would like to extend my deepest gratitude to the presenters of the Tolkien Society 2023 hybrid Seminar, without whom the event would not have happened. I would also like to thank the Society's committee for their continued support in the planning and running of the event, and the publishing of these proceedings. My final thanks go to Francesca Barbini of Luna Press Publishing whose hard work has enabled the publication of this volume. The publication itself is made possible by the generosity of the Peter Roe Memorial Fund, for which I am grateful.

Bibliography

Fimi, Dimitra, *Tolkien, Race and Cultural History: From Fairies to Hobbits* (Basingstoke: Palgrave Macmillan, 2009).

Sherwood, Will, *Eldest and Oldest: Middle-earth's Mother/Father Trees*, February 28, 2025. Available at: https://will-sherwood.com/2025/02/28/middle-earths-mother-father-trees/ [accessed 9 August 2025].

Tolkien, J.R.R., *The Lost Road and Other Writings*, ed. by Christopher Tolkien (London: HarperCollins, 1987).

–– *Unfinished Tales of Númenor and Middle-earth*, ed. by Christopher Tolkien (London: HarperCollins, 1998).

–– *The Lord of the Rings* (London: HarperCollins, 2007).

–– *The Letters of J. R. R. Tolkien: Revised and Expanded edition*, ed. by Humphrey Carpenter with the assistance of Christopher Tolkien (London: HarperCollins, 2023).

Sea Goddess Worship and the Power of the King: Parallel between Aldarion, Uinen, Mataram Sultanate, and Javanese Queen of the Southern Sea

Putri Prihatini

Maritime traditions in various cultures are rooted in people's complicated relationship with the sea. The ocean is both bountiful and terrifying, and its vastness lends great political power to rulers. Many aspects of maritime culture in the world are related to survival, shown by the expressions of gratitude and prayers. However, there are also traditions upheld to express the rule or dominion over maritime expansion and power.

The island kingdom of Númenor has a rich maritime culture, and the exploits of its sixth king, Aldarion, reflects the strong connection between the power of a ruler and the manifestation of the sea in the form of the greatly respected Lady Uinen. This dynamic between Aldarion and Uinen parallels a real-life example from a wildly different cultural reference: the tale of Panembahan Senopati, the first ruler of Mataram Sultanate in Java, and the sea goddess Kanjeng Ratu Kidul which this paper will examine.

1 - Power from the Sea

The image of the daunting sea and its relationship with power is present even in J.R.R. Tolkien's own faith, particularly in the image of Mary as *Stella Maris*, or The Star of the Sea. Marian hymn *Hail, Queen of Heaven, the Ocean Star* by Father John Lingard, which was based on a Medieval hymn *Ave maris stella* ('Hail, Star of the Sea'), invokes the image of Mary as 'Queen of Heaven' and 'the Ocean Star', equating the trials and tribulations of Mankind to tempestuous seas.

The comparison with Tolkien's work is palpable in the Elven hymn of Elbereth. Tolkien himself agreed that the invocations of Elbereth have a connection to the Catholic devotion of Mary:

> I am a Christian (which can be deduced from my stories), and in fact a Roman Catholic. The latter 'fact' perhaps cannot be deduced; though one critic (by letter) asserted that the invocations of Elbereth, and the character of Galadriel as directly described (or through the words of Gimli and Sam) were clearly related to Catholic devotion of Mary. (*Letters*, Letter 213, 288)

Like in the original *Ave Maris Stella* and John Lingard's hymn, Gildor Inglorion and his company of the Elves sing a hymn to Elbereth that depicts her as a "Queen beyond the Western Sea" and "the starlight on the Western Seas" (*FR*, 'Three is Company', 79).

However, the more suitable example of how the power of the sea lends a power legitimacy to a ruling power can be seen in a historical ceremony in Venice called *Sposalizio del Mare*, or the Marriage of the Sea. The ceremony involved the doge of Venice throwing a ring into the Adriatic Sea as a supposed manifestation of Venice's maritime power; a custom continued by the mayor of Venice since its revival. Edward Muir described the ceremony as a form of civic rituals, where the Patriarch of

Venice pronounced the nuptial benedictine to consecrate the ceremony, right before the doge throwing the ring into the sea.

> The essential political point, then, was that in marrying the sea the doge established his legitimate rights of domination over trade routes and over the lands lapped by the waters of the Adriatic. (Muir 1981, 124)

Tolkien's work also provides a more direct example of how the power from the sea lends a powerful legitimacy to Aldarion and rulers of Númenor. Among all the kings of Númenor, Aldarion was responsible for the expansion of Númenor's maritime tradition. One of his notable achievements was the founding of the Guild of Venturers, a brotherhood that consisted of seamen and mariners. They called themselves *Uinendili*, the Lovers of Uinen, showing how the Númenóreans revered Uinen, the Lady of the Seas and one of the servants of Ulmo, indicating a special bond with her. When they were not sailing with Aldarion, their great ship would be anchored off an island called Tol Uinen, said to have been placed there by Uinen herself.

The Númenóreans revered Uinen and sought her protection, for she loved all the sea creatures and the mariners. Uinen affected the life of the Númenóreans and their mariners in a more hands-on, direct way. Aldarion had always realized this, considering his and his mariners' safety depended on her grace. However, the tale of Aldarion and Erendis alludes to a more special bond between Aldarion and Uinen, especially when we also consider the (strained) marriage between Aldarion and Erendis. This special, almost personal bond between them has a surprisingly close parallel in Javanese culture: the legendary tale of Panembahan Senopati of Mataram Sultanate and the mythical sea ruler Kanjeng Ratu Kidul.

2 - The King and the Sea Goddess

The tale of Panembahan Senopati and Kanjeng Ratu Kidul is an enduring legend in Javanese culture, a mixture of history, folklore, and mythology. Their tale was recorded in various versions of a manuscript titled *Babad Tanah Jawi* or 'History of the Land of Java'; a collection of manuscripts that chronicled the history of Javanese kingdoms and royals in a form of macapat, or traditional Javanese verses.

Babad Tanah Jawi has numerous versions, but not one of them is older than the eighteenth century. Despite the title, scholars avoid using *Babad Tanah Jawi* as factual historical accounts, for all versions of the manuscripts mixed folklore, legends, and mythological elements. It has many versions, but historians think that there are at least two master manuscripts, each written in 1722 and 1788.

Despite the different versions, every *Babad Tanah Jawa* manuscript notably mentions the bond between Panembahan Senopati, the first ruler of Mataram Sultanate, and a revered mythological figure called Kanjeng Ratu Kidul, or the Queen of the Southern Sea, whose dominion is believed to be in the Indian Ocean. The verses describe the crucial role of this mythological queen of the sea in making Panembahan Senopati a king. Hans Ras has linked this manuscript to the literary form of power legitimation for the descendants of Panembahan Senopati:

> The motif of the mythical founder of the dynasty and his supernatural bride from whose primeval union their descendants derive their right to rule has been substituted here by Ratu Kidul's permanent marriage to all the successive rulers who were to reign over the whole of Java. The relationship

between the ruling monarchs, from Senapati onwards, and
their supernatural bride is one which needs to be continually
renewed. (1987, 349)

Panembahan Senopati was a historical figure, yet many
depictions of his life incorporate legends and folklore, making
him a unique figure in the manuscript and comparable to
Aldarion, whose chronicle with Erendis, 'The Mariner's Wife',
was Númenor's only internal history that survived the drowning
of the island, as Tolkien described in his letter for Dick Plotz:

This [The Mariner's Wife] is supposed to have been preserved
in the Downfall, when most of Númenórean lore was lost
except that that dealt with the First Age, because it tells how
Númenor became involved in the politics of Middle-earth.
(*Letters*, Letter 276, 360)

Panembahan Senopati's connection with Kanjeng Ratu Kidul
was related to his journey into becoming a new ruler of Java,
following the political strife during the previous era of Pajang
Kingdom, and according to the manuscript, a prophecy that
he would become the king of a kingdom that was even more
powerful than Pajang; legitimizing his power and that of his
descendants.

In *Serat Sri Nata*, a version of *Babad Tanah Jawi* from 1866,
the connection between Panembahan Senopati's prophetic
kingly power and the power of Kanjeng Ratu Kidul was even
declared in the verse that depicted their first encounter on
Parangkusumo Beach:

Ratu Kidul alon matur,
"Sang Nata, nuwun kang sih
Nuwun waluya samodra
Miwah isinipun sami."
Senopati duk miyarsa
Tumungkul pan datan angling.

(Dipomenggolo 2015, 228; I: 1-6)

Queen of the Southern Sea greeted him,
"O, King, take pity
Return the state of this sea
and everything that lives here."
Senopati heard her
Kneeled without words.

(My translation)

One interesting detail here is in the second line, where Kanjeng Ratu Kidul addresses him as 'Sang Nata'. While *nata* itself means guardian, *Sang Nata* is commonly used to address a ruler, as reflected from the title of the manuscript. This scene happens after Senopati performs a meditation on Parangkusumo Beach. His meditation creates an immense supernatural energy that alters the sea: the water rises and becomes hot, almost boiling; the seabed moves, and lightning strikes endlessly. Only when the queen finally appears and addresses him does he stop his meditation and talk to her.

The rest of the verses in this version of the manuscript describe how Panembahan Senopati and Kanjeng Ratu Kidul made oaths after their lovemaking: he and his descendants would be the spiritual consorts of the queen, and in return, she would lend her power to him and his descendants in their time of need. In essence, her presence in these texts symbolize the form of power legitimation to Panembahan Senopati and his descendants. A special bond formed, like how Aldarion asked the favor of Uinen in his seafaring life and the expansion of Númenor's maritime tradition, which marked the major achievements of his ruling period.

While the relationship between Aldarion and Uinen was not described as matrimonial in nature, there are several allusions to their deeper connection, especially when we compare it with the parallel storyline of the strained marriage between Aldarion and Erendis. During a feast when Aldarion's kin dubs her Uinéniel, or Daughter of Uinen, Erendis responds, "call me by no such name! I am no daughter of Uinen: rather she is my foe", for her husband spends more time on his voyages than with her, and by extension what Uinen symbolizes (*UT*, 191). After Erendis invites Aldarion to see the rolling pastures of Emerië, Erendis declares: "I will not share my husband with the Lady Uinen" (191). He counters by saying that Oromë, the Huntsman of the Valar, should have been his enemy too, for both he and Erendis love the trees that grow wild.

Erendis even declares that Aldarion would cut any wood as a gift for Uinen, referring to the numerous trees felled to build his ships. These expressions, while not necessarily literal, show an interesting dynamic between Aldarion and Uinen as the important manifestation of the gracious sea. She grants protection, and in extension, supports Aldarion's goal in expanding Númenor's maritime power, reflected in a mariner's guild that declares themselves The Lovers of Uinen. Aldarion's love for voyage surpasses his marriage to Erendis and shows a level of devotion similar to the connection between Panembahan Senapati and Kanjeng Ratu Kidul.

The ocean is not the only dominion that marks the connection between power and devotion in both Aldarion and Panembahan Senopati's tales. There is an interesting part of the text where Ki Juru, Senopati's loyal follower who later becomes his vice regent, helps him secure spiritual support from Mount Merapi, a volcano that is considered sacred in Javanese culture. This verse shows how, during the time when Senopati needed it, Ki Juru urged him to ask for the Queen of the South Sea and the spirits of Mount Merapi to lend their hands, fulfilling their promises:

Kyai Juru aris mojar,
"Lamun sembada ing karsi
Uni ika asemayan
Kala neng dhasar jeladri
Mangke sedheng tinagih
Pan wus tekeng semayeku.
Kelawan kang Kayangan
Ing Gunung Merapi iki
Sayektine ulun ingkang ndhatengana."

(Dipomenggolo 2015, 262, VIII: 1-9)

Ki Juru declared,
"If you wish,
That old promise
Uttered at the bottom of the sea
It's time to fulfill it
The time has come for it.

As for the one in Heaven
at the top of Mount Merapi
It was thanks to me."

(My translation)

The spiritual connections between the mountain and the sea in *Babad Tanah Jawi* is also reflected in Aldarion's connection with Uinen's dominion and his maritime expansion. They are acknowledged in the forms of codified rituals, which exist in both the realm of Númenor and Javanese culture.

3 - Parallels in Codified Rituals

Tolkien mentions two important rituals among the Númenóreans that had direct connections to the mountain and the sea. The Three Prayers, centered at the peak of Meneltarma, saw the king or queen carrying offerings for Eru in a silent ceremony, sending their gratitude and wishing for protection and prosperity. Aldarion even became the sixth king of Númenor right after *Erukyermë*, or Prayer to Eru, which was the spring ritual.

The other ritual, the Green Bough of Return, was a maritime tradition that involved placing a branch from a fragrant tree at the prow of the ships, which brought good fortune to the sailors and marked their friendship with Uinen and her spouse, Ossë. An interesting connection between the mountain and the sea, especially considering how Manwe and Ulmo, the Valar of the air and the waters, were close in might and had a great friendship, and their dominions such as the air, wind, and water were important in maritime culture.

A similar connection can be found in two important rituals conducted by the Yogyakarta Sultanate, one of the two smaller kingdoms formed after the Treaty of Giyanti in 1775 which split the power of Mataram Sultanate (the other being Surakarta Sunanate) (Sabdacarakatama 2009). Both kingdoms have rituals that center on the mountain and the sea. Every year, Yogyakarta Sultanate conducts ceremonies that center in places with spiritual importance; Labuhan Merapi is conducted in Mount Merapi, while Labuhan Parangkusumo is on the beach where Panembahan Senopati was believed to have encountered Kanjeng Ratu Kidul for the first time.

Both ceremonies involve presenting the offerings for the spiritual rulers of Mount Merapi and the Indian Ocean - reminders of the supposed special spiritual connection between the rulers of Mataram and Yogyakarta and Kanjeng Ratu Kidul. The ceremonies are also intended as wishes for prosperity and protection, and the connection between the rulers and the legendary sea queen are emphasized with the details of the offerings, which include old objects that belonged to the past royals (including hair and nail clippings as parts of their physical bodies), and specific personal items like a selection of fabrics, perfume, and flowers for Kanjeng Ratu Kidul. The hair and nail clippings are buried under the rock where Panembahan Senopati was believed to emerge from the underwater kingdom of Kanjeng Ratu Kidul for the first time, while the queen's gifts are placed on a bamboo raft and cast into the sea. These are done around the same time as offerings being thrown into the cone of Mount Merapi.

The rituals are done to solidify the role of the sea goddess in the forming of royal grounds; an effort to provide power legitimacy for the newly formed small kingdoms after the

Treaty of Giyanti, using rituals as the tangible expressions (Friend 2006, 14). While Tolkien did not elaborate on this aspect, maritime rituals like Green Bough of Return reflect a similar theme because it symbolizes the special relationship between the Númenóreans and Uinen.

In conclusion, while Númenor was a kingdom with a strong maritime culture, the significant relationship between Aldarion and Uinen - and what she manifests - reflects the power legitimation lent by the spiritual representation of the sea. The fact that their relationship parallels that between the legendary king and a mythological goddess of the sea mentioned in a Javanese manuscript proves an intriguing and interesting cultural connection based on both the important and dangerous power of the sea.

Bibliography

Anon., *Ave Maris Stella: Hail Star of the Ocean*, Available at: <http://www.preces-latinae.org/thesaurus/BVM/AveMarisStella.html> [Accessed 15 September 2023]

Anon., *Serat Sri Nata: Babad Tanah Jawi*, translated and transcribed by Anton Suparnjo Dipomenggolo, (Yogyakarta: Penerbit Elmatera, 2015).

Friend, Maria, 'Kanjeng Ratu Kidul, the Elusive Goddess of Java', *TAASA Review*, 15. 4 (2006), pp. 14-15.

Lingard, John, *Hail, Queen of Heaven, the Ocean Star*, Available at: <https://hymnary.org/text/hail_queen_of_heaven_the_ocean_star> [Accessed 15 September 2023]

Muir, Edward, *Civic Ritual in Renaissance Venice*, (New Jersey: Princeton University Press, 1981).

Ras, J.J., 'The Genesis of the Babad Tanah Jawi; Origin and Function of the Javanese Court Chronicle', *Bijdragen tot de Taal-, Land- en Volkenkunde / Journal of the Humanities and Social Sciences of Southeast Asia and Oceania*, 143. 2 (1987), p. 349.

Sabdacarakatama, *Sejarah Keraton Yogyakarta*, (Yogyakarta: Narasi, 2009).

Tolkien, J.R.R., *Unfinished Tales*, ed. by Christopher Tolkien (New York: Del Rey, 1980).

— *The Letters of J.R.R. Tolkien*, ed. by Humphrey Carpenter with the assistance of Christopher Tolkien (London: HarperCollins, 2000).

— *The Lord of the Rings: The Fellowship of the Ring*, (Massachusetts: Houghton Mifflin Harcourt, 2004).

Penguasa Laut dan Sang Raja:
Paralel antara Aldarion, Uinen, Kesultanan
Mataram, dan Ratu Laut Selatan Jawa

Putri Prihatini

Tradisi maritim di berbagai negara berakar dari hubungan erat masyarakat dengan lautan. Samudra yang kaya-raya, menakutkan, sekaligus luas pun menjadi sumber kekuatan politik bagi para penguasa. Berbagai aspek budaya maritim di dunia terkait erat dengan kehidupan sehari-hari dan strategi bertahan hidup, seperti yang terlihat dari berbagai ekspresi syukur serta ritual doa. Akan tetapi, ada juga tradisi yang diciptakan sebagai ekspresi kuasa terhadap kekuatan serta ekspansi maritim.

Kerajaan Númenor memiliki budaya maritim yang kental, dan kisah hidup Aldarion, rajanya yang keenam, menunjukkan adanya hubungan erat antara penguasa dan manifestasi kekuatan samudra yang terwujud dalam sosok Lady Uinen yang dihormati oleh penduduk Númenor. Tulisan ini akan membahas dinamika relasi antara Aldarion dan Uinen mencerminkan referensi budaya yang sepintas berbeda jauh tetapi memiliki kesamaan, yaitu kisah Panembahan Senopati, penguasa pertama Kesultanan Mataram di Jawa, serta Kanjeng Ratu Kidul sang penguasa Laut Selatan.

1 - Kuasa dari Samudra

Bayangan akan samudra yang ganas serta kaitannya dengan kekuasaan tidak hanya hadir dalam kebudayaan dunia, tetapi juga kepercayaan J.R.R. Tolkien sendiri, terutama dalam imaji Bunda Maria sebagai *Stella Maris* atau Bintang Samudra. Himne Maria yang berjudul *Hail, Queen of Heaven, the Ocean Star* gubahan Fr. John Lingard, diciptakan berdasarkan himne Abad Pertengahan Ave maris stella, merefleksikan citra Maria sebagai 'Ratu di Surga' dan 'Bintang Samudra' serta menyamakan lautan yang bergejolak dengan cobaan yang dihadapi umat manusia di dunia.

Perbandingan ini semakin terlihat dalam salah satu sajak gubahan Tolkien: himne kaum Elf untuk Elbereth. Tolkien sendiri menyebut bahwa puja-puji terhadap Elbereth dalam sajak tersebut mirip dengan devosi Katolik untuk Maria:

> *I am a Christian (which can be deduced from my stories), and in fact a Roman Catholic. The latter 'fact' perhaps cannot be deduced; though one critic (by letter) asserted that the invocations of Elbereth, and the character of Galadriel as directly described (or through the words of Gimli and Sam) were clearly related to Catholic devotion of Mary.* (*Letters*, Letter 213, 288)

Aku penganut Kristen (bisa disimpulkan dari karya-karyaku), tepatnya Katolik Roma. Fakta yang terakhir itu mungkin tidak bisa disimpulkan begitu saja; tetapi salah satu kritikus (lewat surat) menegaskan bahwa puja-puji untuk Elbereth serta karakter Galadriel seperti yang kugambarkan (atau lewat ujaran Gimli dan Sam) punya kaitan jelas dengan devosi Katolik terhadap Maria. (Terjemahan sendiri)

Seperti Ave Maris Stella dan himne karya John Lingard, Gildor Inglorion dan para Elf menyanyikan himne kepada Elbereth serta membayangkannya sebagai "Ratu di Seberang Laut Barat" serta "cahaya bintang di atas Laut Barat" (*FR*, 'Three is Company', 79).

Akan tetapi, contoh yang lebih mendekati terkait laut sebagai dasar legitimasi kekuatan untuk penguasa terlihat dari upacara kuno di Venesia bernama *Sposalizio del Mare*, Pernikahan Laut. Dalam upacara ini, sang doge melemparkan cincin ke Laut Adriatik sebagai lambang kekuatan maritim Venesia; ritual yang dipertahankan oleh walikota Venesia masa kini sejak upacara tersebut dihidupkan kembali. Edward Muir menggambarkan upacara tersebut sebagai bentuk tradisi kemasyarakatan (civic rituals), di mana sang Patriark Venesia mendeklarasikan pemberkatan pernikahan untuk mentahbiskan upacara tersebut, tepat sebelum sang doge melemparkan cincin ke laut.

The essential political point, then, was that in marrying the sea the doge established his legitimate rights of domination over trade routes and over the lands lapped by the waters of the Adriatic. (Muir 1981, 124)

Makna politisnya adalah bahwa dengan menikahi laut, sang doge telah mengesahkan kuasanya terhadap dominasi jalur-jalur perdagangan serta semua negeri yang berbatasan dengan perairan Adriatik. (Terjemahan sendiri)

Karya Tolkien juga memiliki contoh terkait bagaimana kekuasan atas laut memberikan kekuatan politik bagi Aldarion sebagai penguasa Númenor. Dibandingkan para raja Númenor,

Aldarion adalah yang pertama kali melebarkan tradisi maritim Númenor. Salah satu pencapaiannya adalah pembentukan the Guild of Venturers, sebuah kelompok persaudaraan yang terdiri dari para pelaut. Mereka menyebut diri mereka Uinendili, para Kekasih Uinen; sebuah bentuk rasa hormat kaum Númenor terhadap sang Ratu Laut serta simbol ikatan istimewa mereka dengannya. Ketika mereka sedang tidak berlayar bersama Aldarion, para Uinendili menambatkan kapal besar mereka di Tol Uinen, sebuah pulau yang konon ditempatkan sendiri oleh Uinen di perairan tersebut.

Kaum Númenor menghormati Uinen dan senantiasa mencari perlindungannya karena dia mencintai semua makhluk samudra serta para pelaut. Uinen berperan langsung dalam kehidupan kaum Númenor dan para pelaut mereka. Aldarion yang menyadari hal ini pun menyandarkan keselamatannya serta para pelautnya kepada kemurahan hati Uinen. Kisah Aldarion dan istrinya, Erendis, justru semakin menunjukkan ikatan yang kedudukannya jauh lebih istimewa antara sang raja dan Uinen, apalagi melihat ketegangan dalam hubungan pernikahan Aldarion dan Erendis. Uniknya, ikatan istimewa antara Aldarion dan Uinen ini memiliki paralel erat dengan kisah serupa dalam kultur Jawa: legenda Panembahan Senopati dari Kesultanan Mataram dan penguasa laut Kanjeng Ratu Kidul.

2 - Sang Raja and Dewi Laut

Kisah Panembahan Senopati dan Kanjeng Ratu Kidul sangat terkenal dalam budaya Jawa dan memadukan sejarah, folklor, serta mitologi. Kisah mereka terekam dalam berbagai versi manuskrip *Babad Tanah Jawi* ('Sejarah Tanah Jawa'); sebuah koleksi manuskrip yang merekam sejarah berbagai kerajaan serta para penguasa kuno Jawa dalam bentuk sajak macapat.

Babad Tanah Jawi memiliki banyak versi, tetapi tidak ada yang lebih tua dari abad kedelepan belas. Akademisi menghindari penggunaan *Babad Tanah Jawi* sebagai dokumen sejarah murni karena semua versinya memadukan elemen folklor, legenda, dan mitologi. Menurut para sejarawan, *Babad Tanah Jawi* kemungkinan memiliki setidaknya dua manuskrip sumber, masing-masing ditulis pada tahun 1772 dan 1788.

Walau banyak versi berbeda, setiap manuskrip *Babad Tanah Jawi* menyebutkan kisah ikatan antara Panembahan Senopati, penguasa pertama Kesultanan Mataram, dengan sosok Kanjeng Ratu Kidul atau Ratu Laut Selatan, yang dipercaya menguasai Samudra Hindia. Lirik-lirik dalam manuskrip tersebut mengisahkan peran penting sang ratu dalam menjadikan Panembahan Senopati raja. Hans Ras memandang manuskrip ini sebagai bentuk tertulis dari legitimasi kekuasaan yang juga dimiliki keturunan Panembahan Senopati:

The motif of the mythical founder of the dynasty and his supernatural bride from whose primeval union their descendants derive their right to rule has been substituted here by Ratu Kidul's permanent marriage to all the successive rulers who were to reign over the whole of Java. The relationship between the ruling monarchs, from Senapati onwards, and their supernatural bride is one which needs to be continually renewed. (1987, 349)

Motif utama dari mitos sang pendiri dinasti serta mempelai supernatural yang memberinya hak memerintah lewat pernikahan suci mereka telah digantikan oleh pernikahan abadi Ratu Kidul dengan generasi penguasa seterusnya yang menguasai seluruh Jawa. Hubungan antara penguasa kerajaan dengan sang mempelai supernatural yang diawali dari Senopati pun menjadi sesuatu yang harus terus dilakukan. (Terjemahan sendiri)

Panembahan Senopati adalah figur historis, tetapi berbagai versi kisah hidupnya bercampur dengan legenda dan folklor, sesuatu yang menjadikannya sosok unik dalam Babad Tanah Jawi. Hal ini semakin memperjelas koneksinya dengan Aldarion, yang kisahnya bersama Erendis terangkum dalam *Istri Sang Pelaut* (*The Mariner's Wife*), satu-satunya hikayat sejarah internal Númenor yang selamat dari tenggelamnya pulau tersebut, seperti yang ditulis Tolkien dalam suratnya untuk Dick Plotz:

This [The Mariner's Wife] is supposed to have been preserved in the Downfall, when most of Númenórean lore was lost except that that dealt with the First Age, because it tells how Númenor became involved in the politics of Middle-earth. (*Letters*, Letter 276, 360)

Kisah ini [Istri Sang Pelaut] selamat dari perisriwa Kejatuhan, di mana sebagian besar kisah tentang Númenor lenyap kecuali yang berasal dari Zaman Pertama, karena kisah-kisah itulah yang menggambarkan bagaimana Númenór mulai terlibat dalam politik Middle-earth. (Terjemahan sendiri)

Hubungan Panembahan Senopati dan Kanjeng Ratu Kidul terkait dengan perjalanannya untuk menjadi penguasa baru di Jawa menyusul kekacauan politik yang terjadi di era Kerajaan Pajang. Manuskrip Babad Tanah Jawi menyebut ramalan tentang Panembahan Senopati yang akan menjadi penguasa kerajaan yang bahkan lebih kuat daripada Pajang. Hal ini memberi legitimasi atas kekuasaannya serta para penerusnya.

Dalam *Serat Sri Nata*, salah satu versi *Babad Tanah Jawi* dari tahun 1866, kaitan akan janji kuasa Panembahan Senopati sebagai raja dengan kekuatan Kanjeng Ratu Kidul tergambar dalam bait berisi pertemuan pertama keduanya di Pantai Parangkusumo:

Ratu Kidul alon matur,
"Sang Nata, nuwun kang sih
Nuwun waluya samodra
Miwah isinipun sami."
Senopati duk miyarsa
Tumungkul pan datan angling.

(Dipomenggolo 2015, 228; I: 1-6)

Ratu Selatan pelan berkata
"Hai baginda, kasihanilah
Kembalikanlah lautan ini
Dan semua isinya."
Senopati ketika mendengar
Tunduk tanpa berkata.

(Terjemahan Dipomenggolo)

Yang menarik dari bait ini adalah baris kedua, di mana Kanjeng Ratu Kidul memanggil Panembahan Senopati dengan sebutan Sang Nata, yang biasanya ditujukan kepada penguasa. Pertemuan ini terjadi setelah Senopati bermeditasi di Parangkusumo. Meditasinya menciptakan energi supernatural yang begitu besar sehingga mempengaruhi kondisi lautan: permukaan laut naik dan suhunya menjadi lebih panas, nyaris mendidih; dasar laut bergejolak, dan petir melanda berkali-kali. Meditasinya baru berhenti ketika sang ratu akhirnya muncul dan memanggil namanya.

Bait-bait selanjutnya mendeskripsikan sumpah antara Panembahan Senopati dan Kanjeng Ratu Kidul yang mereka buat setelah memadu kasih. Panembahan Senopati dan para penerusnya akan menjadi pasangan spiritual sang ratu, dan sebagai gantinya, sang ratu akan meminjamkan kekuatannya kepada Panembahan Senopati dan penerusnya ketika mereka membutuhkannya. Kehadiran sang ratu dalam teks ini menyimbolkan bentuk legitimasi kekuasaan untuk Panembahan Senopati dan penerusnya. Hubungan istimewa ini juga tercermin pada kisah Aldarion yang memohon berkat Uinen demi pelayaran serta ekspansi kekuasaan maritim Númenor, sesuatu yang menjadi pencapaian utama selama pemerintahannya.

Walau hubungan antara Aldarion dan Uinen tidak bersifat marital, ada beberapa bagian yang mendeskripsikan sifat hubungan yang lebih istimewa, terutama jika kita membandingkannya dengan pernikahan Aldarion dan Erendis yang kurang harmonis. Misalnya, ketika kerabat Aldarion memanggil Erendis dengan nama Uinéniel atau Putri Uinen, Erendis merespons, "Jangan panggil aku dengan nama itu! Aku bukan putri Uinen; dia adalah musuhku." Hal ini karena Aldarion menghabiskan waktu lebih lama berlayar daripada bersama Erendis (*UT*, 191, terjemahan sendiri). Setelah Erendis mengundang Aldarion untuk melihat padang rumput luas di Emerië, dia berkata, "Aku tidak akan membagi suamiku dengan Lady Uinen" (191). Aldarion membalas dengan menyebut bahwa Oromë, sang Pemburu di antara para Valar, seharusnya juga adalah musuhnya, karena dia dan Erendis menyukai pepohonan yang tumbuh liar.

Erendis juga menyebut bahwa Aldarion tidak akan segan menebang pohon sebagai hadiah untuk Uinen, merujuk pada praktik penebangan pohon untuk membangun kapal. Walau semua pernyataan ini tidak bersifat harfiah, mereka menunjukkan dinamika menarik antara Aldarion dan Uinen yang menjadi manifestasi dari lautan. Uinen memberi perlindungan dan mendukung misi Aldarion dalam mengembangkan kekuatan maritim Númenor, sesuatu yang dicerminkan oleh para pelaut yang menyebut diri mereka Para Kekasih Uinen. Kecintaan Aldarion terhadap pelayaran melebihi perasaannya terhadap istrinya, Erendis; sebuah tingkat pengabdian yang mirip dengan hubungan antara Panembahan Senopati dan Kanjeng Ratu Kidul.

Laut bukan satu-satunya area yang menunjukkan hubungan antara kekuasaan dan pengabdian dalam kisah Aldarion serta Panembahan Senopati. Ada bait menarik di mana Ki Juru, pengikut setia Panembahan Senopati yang kemudian menjadi patihnya, membantu Panembahan Senopati mendapatkan dukungan spiritual dari Gunung Merapi, gunung berapi yang dianggap sakral dalam budaya Jawa. Bait tersebut mengisahkan bagaimana Ki Juru mendesak Panembahan Senopati menagih janji terhadap Ratu Laut Selatan dan para penghuni Gunung Merapi untuk membantunya:

Kyai Juru aris mojar,
"Lamun sembada ing karsi
Uni ika asemayan
Kala neng dhasar jeladri
Mangke sedheng tinagih

Pan wus tekeng semayeku.
Kelawan kang Kayangan
Ing Gunung Merapi iki
Sayektine ulun ingkang ndhatengana."

(Dipomenggolo 2015, 262; VIII: 1-9)

Ki Juru berkata,
"Kalau selaras dengan kehendak
Dulu itu perjanjian
Waktu di dasar laut
Sekarang saatnya ditagih
Sudah tiba saat perjanjian itu
Dengan yang di Kayangan
Di Gunung Merapi ini
Sebenarnya saya yang mendatangkan."

(Terjemahan Dipomenggolo)

Koneksi spiritual antara gunung dan laut dalam *Babad Tanah Jawi* juga tercermin dalam hubungan Aldarion dan ekspansi maritimnya dengan wilayah kekuasaan Uinen. Hal ini terlihat dari ritual khusus yang ada di Númenor maupun dalam Jawa budaya.

3 - Paralel dalam Ritual

Tolkien menyebut dua jenis ritual di Númenor yang berhubungan langsung dengan gunung serta laut. Dalam Tiga Doa (*The Three Prayers*), ritual yang dilakukan di puncak Meneltarma, sang raja atau ratu membawa persembahan untuk Eru dalam keheningan sebagai perwujudan rasa syukur serta doa untuk perlindungan dan kemakmuran. Aldarion bahkan dinobatkan menjadi raja Númenor keenam tepat setelah *Erukyermë* (Doa kepada Eru), upacara musim semi dalam rangkaian ritual tersebut.

Ritual lainnya, Dahan Hijau Kepulangan (the Green Bough of Return), adalah tradisi maritim yang melibatkan peletakan dahan pohon wangi pada haluan kapal, sesuatu yang dipercaya membawa keberuntungan bagi para pelaut serta tanda persahabatan mereka dengan Uinen dan pasangannya, Ossë. Koneksi antara gunung dan laut dalam ritual ini menarik, terutama melihat eratnya persahabatan antara Manwë dan Ulmo, Valar yang menguasai udara dan laut. Elemen kekuasaan mereka seperti udara, angin, dan air juga penting dalam budaya maritim.

Koneksi antar tradisi terlihat jelas dari dua ritual tahunan Kesultanan Yogyakarta, salah satu dari dua kerajaan kecil yang terbentuk lewat Perjanjian Giyanti pada tahun 1775, yang memecah wilayah kekuasaan Kesultanan Mataram (satu lagi adalah Kasunanan Surakarta) (Sabdacarakatama 2009). Kedua kerajaan ini memiliki ritual yang berpusat pada gunung dan lautan. Setiap tahun, Kesultanan Yogyakarta melaksanakan upacara Labuhan Merapi di Gunung Merapi dan Labuhan Parangkusumo di Pantai Parangkusumo, tempat di mana Panembahan Senopati dipercaya bertemu Kanjeng Ratu Kidul untuk pertama kalinya.

Kedua upacara tersebut melibatkan sesaji untuk para pemimpin spiritual di Gunung Merapi dan Samudra Hindia, pengingat akan koneksi spiritual antara penguasa Mataram dan Yogyakarta dengan Kanjeng Ratu Kidul. Upacara tersebut juga merupakan permohohan akan kemakmuran dan perlindungan, dan hubungan antara penguasa kerajaan dengan ratu laut terlihat dari rincian sesaji, termasuk benda-benda lama milik para penguasa sebelumnya (misalnya helai rambut dan potongan kuku) serta hadiah khusus untuk Kanjeng Ratu Kidul seperti kain batik, parfum, dan bunga. Rambut dan kuku dikubur di bawah batu tempat Panembahan Senopati dipercaya muncul dari kerajaan bawah laut milik Kanjeng Ratu Kidul, sedangkan hadiah sang ratu diletakkan di rakit bambu dan dilarung. Hal ini dilakukan pada waktu yang kurang lebih sama dengan pelemparan sesaji ke kawah Merapi.

Semua ritual ini menegaskan peran sang dewi laut dalam kerajaan, yaitu memberikan legitimasi bagi kerajaan-kerajaan kecil yang terbentuk setelah Perjanjian Giyanti, lengkap dengan ritual sebagai perwujudan nyatanya (Friends 2006, 14). Tolkien mungkin tidak menjabarkan detail serupa, tetapi ritual maritim seperti *Green Bough of Return* mencerminkan tema serupa karena menyimbolkan hubungan istimewa antara kaum Númenor dan Uinen.

Kesimpulannya, walau Númenor merupakan kerajaan dengan tradisi maritim yang kuat, hubungan istimewa antara Aldarion dan Uinen serta makna di baliknya mencerminkan legitimasi kekuasaan yang tercermin dari representasi spiritual lautan. Fakta bahwa hal ini memiliki paralel dengan penguasa legendaris dan dewi laut dalam manuskrip Jawa menunjukkan adanya koneksi antarbudaya yang menarik terkait pemahaman akan kekuatan laut yang penting sekaligus berbahaya.

Daftar Pustaka

Anon., *Ave Maris Stella: Hail Star of the Ocean*, Available at: <http://www.preces-latinae.org/thesaurus/BVM/AveMarisStella.html> [Accessed 15 September 2023]

Anon., *Serat Sri Nata: Babad Tanah Jawi*, translated and transcribed by Anton Suparnjo Dipomenggolo, (Yogyakarta: Penerbit Elmatera, 2015).

Friend, Maria, 'Kanjeng Ratu Kidul, the Elusive Goddess of Java', *TAASA Review*, 15. 4 (2006), pp. 14-15.

Lingard, John, *Hail, Queen of Heaven, the Ocean Star*, Available at: <https://hymnary.org/text/hail_queen_of_heaven_the_ocean_star> [Accessed 15 September 2023]

Muir, Edward, *Civic Ritual in Renaissance Venice*, (New Jersey: Princeton University Press, 1981).

Ras, J.J., 'The Genesis of the Babad Tanah Jawi; Origin and Function of the Javanese Court Chronicle', *Bijdragen tot de Taal-, Land- en Volkenkunde / Journal of the Humanities and Social Sciences of Southeast Asia and Oceania*, 143. 2 (1987), p. 349.

Sabdacarakatama, *Sejarah Keraton Yogyakarta*, (Yogyakarta: Narasi, 2009).

Tolkien, J.R.R., *Unfinished Tales*, ed. by Christopher Tolkien (New York: Del Rey, 1980).

—— *The Letters of J.R.R. Tolkien*, ed. by Humphrey Carpenter with the assistance of Christopher Tolkien (London: HarperCollins, 2000).

—— *The Lord of the Rings: The Fellowship of the Ring*, (Massachusetts: Houghton Mifflin Harcourt, 2004).

Dealing with the Dead: Nuances of ancient Egypt and medieval theology in Númenor

Irina Metzler

How a society disposes of the bodies of its dead can inform greatly about the culture, beliefs, and customs. After all, burial archaeology is the most informative branch of the discipline in our real world. How the Númenóreans and their cultural descendants in Gondor dealt with the bodies of their deceased tells us an enormous amount about them, both from the perspective of us as readers of the stories of the Second Age, and from the point of historic analysis of likely influences on Tolkien's development of his ideas around the funerary practices of Númenor. This is where the preservation of dead bodies, as known from ancient Egypt, and the comparative disregard of the buried body in medieval Christianity come into play. Egyptian mummification did everything possible to preserve the physical body, but medieval theology more or less disregarded physical remains as inconsequential - unless dealing with the venerated bodies of saints of course.

This paper will, firstly, catalogue the evidence for notions of physical incorruptibility and preservation of the cadaver in Tolkien's writings, arranged by the internal time-line of Middle-earth rather than by date of writing or publication, before, secondly, comparing such notions with real-world medieval funerary practices.

1 - Númenor

In the description of the island of Númenor given in *The Silmarillion*, the tall and steep mountain called Meneltarma is at the centre, and at its feet the Númenóreans built their royal tombs (261). Further information tells us that there was a road towards Meneltarma which went into a shallow valley. This was called Noirinan signifying "Valley of the Tombs", because of the rock-cut underground chambers at the head of the valley for deceased rulers (*UT*, 166). Under the Númenórean kings a slow moral decline becomes ever more evident, but the real rot appears to set in during the days of King Tar-Ancalimon. Then

> the fear of death grew ever darker upon them, and they delayed it by all means they could; and they began to build great houses for their dead, while their wise men laboured unceasingly to discover if they might the secret of recalling life, or at least of the prolonging of Men's days. Yet they achieved only the art of preserving incorrupt the dead flesh of Men, and they filled all the land with silent tombs in which the thought of death was enshrined in the darkness. (*Silmarillion*, 266)

In a letter from 1951 addressed to Milton Waldman, Tolkien explained a little more how he saw the Númenórean thanatophobia develop into moral turpitude: "the desire to escape death produced a cult of the dead, and they lavished wealth and art on tombs and memorials" (*Letters*, Letter 131, 155). By the time of Ar-Pharazôn the Golden (3255 S.A.), last king of the island empire, twenty-four deceased Númenórean rulers "slept now in their deep tombs under the mountain of Meneltarma, lying upon beds of gold" (*FoN*, 170). Then in the last days of Númenor, under the rule of Ar-Pharazôn, the Númenóreans in effect colonised areas of Middle-earth, with moral decline reaching an absolute nadir, down to human sacrifice performed on their altars of captured men of Middle-earth, in temples which they had built in their fortresses, together with "great tombs" (*Silmarillion*, 274).

The corruption of Númenor and its last king notably came about through the influence of Sauron. In his guise as Annatar, Sauron tempted not just the Elven smiths of Eregion, who wished to preserve life in Middle-earth, but the Númenóreans and finally Ar-Pharazôn, which enabled him to corrupt the whole Númenórean culture. Sauron's prime instrument was playing on the human fear of dying. Dying is the Gift of Eru to Men but Morgoth changed Men's notion of death from a gift to a curse. Seeing that the Elves were not dying, Men came to think that this was the only distinguishing criterion between the otherwise physically similar Elves and Men. So instead of receiving a divine gift, immortal life had been taken away from Men. This belief might explain the Númenórean desire to prolong their life in the hope they might become elf-like near-immortals again. To all intents and purposes Sauron appears to give them what they want, but it is appearance only, resulting in the hubris of their downfall.

2 - Gondor

There is more information on the afterlife of Númenórean burial practices in Gondor. When Frodo is hosted by Faramir in Ithilien during a brief respite in the quest of the Ring, Faramir tells Frodo (and us, the reader) some more of the back-story of the kingdom of Gondor. The Gondorians, like the Númenóreans hungered after endless life unchanging. Kings made tombs more splendid than houses of the living, and counted old names in the rolls of their descent dearer than the names of sons. Childless lords sat in aged halls musing on heraldry; in secret chambers withered men compounded strong elixirs. (*TT*, 'The Window on the West', 678)

Later in the tale Denethor orders his servants to pick up the body of Faramir, who is burning from a fever, and commands that there is to be no tomb for him and his son Faramir. Instead of being embalmed for a "long slow sleep of death", as would have been the practice appropriate for a Gondorian ruler, they are to '"burn like heathen kings before ever a ship sailed hither from the West'" (*RK*, 'The Siege of Gondor', 825). The fever burning Faramir is perhaps the premonition of real death by immolation in the flames of this threatened funeral pyre. The premature funerary procession then winds its way to a door called Fen Hollen, so called because it was always closed unless for a funeral (826). The burial site for the Gondorian kings and the stewards that followed them echoes its Númenórean predecessor, being also located below the summit of a mountain, here Mindolluin rather than Meneltarma (826). These burials are like mansions, "the houses and domed tombs of bygone kings and lords" (*RK*, 'Minas Tirith', 752). Denethor and Faramir process down the mountainside to Rath Dínen, meaning the Silent Street, which winds "between pale domes and empty halls and images of men long dead […] And dimly to be seen were many rows of tables, carved of marble, and upon each table lay a sleeping form, hands folded, head pillowed upon stone" (*RK*, 'The Siege of Gondor', 826). At this point Denethor breaks with tradition, and refuses to send for the customary embalmers (826). Pat Reynolds quite firmly states that the figures were embalmed bodies, not sculptures, and believes Tolkien deliberately placed Denethor's wish for self-immolation in contrast to the preservation of previous dead (2016, 7). However, Wayne Hammond and Christina Scull note that the "sleeping forms" are ambiguous, as they could either "be effigies, or the embalmed bodies of former Stewards" (2005, 551). They furthermore draw attention to a further funerary reference in the Appendices to the *Lord of the Rings* which relates to the death of Aragorn. Knowing his time had come, Aragorn went to the burial mansion for the kings in Rath Dínen and voluntarily lay down on the "long bed that had been prepared for him" (*RK*, 'Appendix A', 1062). Aragorn falls into sleep with Arwen holding his hand.

> Then a great beauty was revealed in him, so that all who after came there looked on him in wonder, for they saw that the grace of his youth, and the valour of his manhood, and the wisdom and majesty of his age were blended together. And long there he lay, an image of the splendour of the Kings of Men in glory undimmed before the breaking of the world. (1063)

Aragorn's submission to his destiny is written in a positive light by Tolkien (Hammond and Scull 2005, 701). In a draft letter from 1954, Tolkien elucidated that "a good Númenórean died of free will when he felt it to be time to do so" (*Letters*, Letter 156, 205), hence by emulating this Aragorn designates himself as an exemplary man who "would or should *die* voluntarily by surrender with trust *before being compelled*" (*Letters*, Letter 212, 286; emphasis original). In true medieval fashion of the *ars moriendi*, 'the art of dying well', Aragorn, the harbinger of a revived kingdom, dies the good death in contrast to the later kings of Númenor and Gondor who hankered vainly after everlasting life.

3 - Gondor and Egypt

By now the observant reader may be aware of a number of similarities between Númenórean and Gondorian funerary beliefs and practices with those of Egypt and the Near East. As John Garth notes: "Tolkien planted numerous flags of biblical portent in his story of Númenor. […] In Gondor, the Egyptian obsession with mortuary architecture continues" (2020, 41). For one, the kings of Númenor were blessed with a positively Methusalean longevity, but like the pharaohs of ancient Egypt they were more preoccupied with their funerary monuments than with their royal residences. Tolkien had of course alluded to the Egyptian connections himself. In a letter from 1958 to Rhona Bere he explained: "the Númenóreans of Gondor were proud, peculiar, and archaic, and I think are best pictured in (say) Egyptian terms. In many ways they resembled 'Egyptians' - the love of, and power to construct, the gigantic and massive. And in their great interest in ancestry and tombs" (*Letters*, Letter 211, 281). As with so many of Tolkien's writings, the devil is in the detail, as it is the small, little detailed descriptions and mise-en-scène that bring the atmosphere of Middle-earth to life, which here ironically relate to the sites of the dead. The Númenórean and Gondorian obsession with monumental tombs echo Ancient Egypt even down to the location of these burials. Both the Noirinan in Númenor and Rath Dínen in Minas Tirith are in a similar mountainside location to the Egyptian Valley of the Kings (Garth 2020, 143; Smith 2015, 2). And mountains as such share a sacred aspect with pyramids. Meneltarma on Númenor and Mindolluin in Gondor are 'high places' in a religious sense, hence the practice of burying the dead in close proximity, as in at the feet or roots of the holy mountains. Egyptian pyramids can be seen to emulate mountains, by trying to reach for the sacred sky, as did (in) famously the Tower of Babel. What is perhaps less well-known is a recent insight from Egyptology, namely that even after the trend for erecting artificial mountains, that is pyramids, came about, hills or rocks in naturally-occurring pyramidal shape, so-called 'natural pyramids', were used by the Egyptians in relation to tombs (Ejsmond 2018, 169). Like the Egyptians, the Númenóreans and Gondorians projected their beliefs onto the landscape for the purpose of demonstrating status (burial of royalty and nobility) and expressing religious symbolism.

4 – Tolkien's late writings

In a text on typescript covering five sides of four sheets of exam script pages, dated on internal evidence to around 1957-1968, Tolkien jotted down his thoughts on the interaction between body and soul. This passage is worth quoting at length since the notions therein bridge the conceptual gap between religious beliefs in Middle-earth and medieval theology.

> But man-bodies deserted by the *fëa* perish swiftly. They are made to be the houses of *fëar* that, once they are severed from the body, *never return*. The body then has no function (and the shock of the separation is greater); and for the most part it soon decays and passes away into Arda.*
>
> *Not always. Men report that the bodies of some of their Dead long maintain their coherence, and even sometimes endure in fair form as if they slept only. That this is true the Elves know

by proof; but the purpose or reason is not to them clear. Men say that it is the bodies of the holy that sometimes remain long incorrupt: meaning those of whom the *fëar* were strong and yet were turned ever towards Eru in love and hope. This endurance of the body they believe, therefore, to be a sign from Eru for the increase of hope. For men, even more than the Elves, abhor the sight of decay. (*Nature*, 273)

In the appendix on metaphysical and theological themes covered in Tolkien's late writings the editor, Carl F. Hostetter, then adds a couple of explanatory passages on the theme of incorruptibility of the flesh and the so-called odour of sanctity, known to anyone familiar with the Catholic faith, according to which the bodies of holy people are said to emit a fragrant smell, generally likened to flowers (410-1). With this observation it is time to leave the world of the legendarium and turn to medieval and other real-world dealings with the dead.

5 - Medieval eschatology

Medieval preoccupations with death, dying and the correct treatment of the cadaver tended to distinguish not so much between the status of people in this life (lords versus peasants), as with the effects of spiritual states and moral behaviours on the bodies of the dead. To the medieval religious person, paradise was an aspirational condition which mirrored the real, sublunar world, but in which everything - including the human body - had been perfected, so that there was no longer any illness, nobody suffered from hunger, and putrefaction and corporeal corruptibility had ceased. The medieval notion of Paradise was a dream of permanent embalming, [...] of the blessed, of the incorruptibility of the flesh, of itself mortal and perishable. The embalming of corpses reflected this search for permanence and renewal through rebirth. It was an ancient dream that the human world vainly sought to propitiate by simulating the appearance of longevity in the cadavers of the famous, 'treating' them according to certain funerary recipes. (Camporesi 1988, 25)

But embalming is a human craft, an artifice. According to medieval Christian beliefs, true corporeal incorruptibility came about through spiritual virtue, and was divinely granted to those who had lived saintly lives. Below is a random sample of saintly relics, taken from a book published around the time Tolkien was himself in the midst of his academic career, and composing the bulk of his writings, in other words something typical of scholarly interpretation of Tolkien's own time, rather than imposing our contemporary angle.

The bodies of the Saints remained uncorrupted after death. St. Cuthbert's body after eleven years was found 'whole as if it had been alive, with the joints pliable, more like one asleep than a dead person'. [...] Four hundred and eighteen years later the body was again examined and found to be free from corruption. In 1102 the tomb of Edward the Confessor was opened. The body was not decayed, the limbs were flexible. [...] The body of St. Etheldreda was found uncorrupted sixteen years after her death, and a wound in her neck which had been open at her burial was healed, so that nothing but the scar remained. When the body of St. Stephen was discovered an exceedingly sweet smell came from the coffin. (Edwards 1930, 165-6)

Note that St Etheldreda's scar remained - only the saints and martyrs in heaven carried the physical signs of their martyrdom on their bodies, and everyone else including the physically disabled would be resurrected in bodily perfection (Metzler 2006, 55-8).

The medieval theological idea of physical perfection in heaven for all those resurrected appears to be based on a series of biblical passages. There is a verse in the Old Testament that God will not suffer his holy one, who according to prophecy is Jesus, to witness corruption of things mortal (Psalms 16:10). From this passage medieval theologians deduced that God would not suffer his saints to look on decomposition. The idea was then further extrapolated via St Peter in the New Testament to state that Christ's flesh itself did not see corruption (Acts 2:32). Finally, the whole body (*corpus totum*) was also an uncorrupted body (*corpus incorruptum*), at least as far as the bodies of the saints were concerned (Angenendt 1993, 362).[1] St Anselm (born 1033) extrapolated even further that the bodies of anyone entering heaven are also whole and uncorrupted. Anyone becoming one of the elect and entering heaven would have to be very similar to the saints, anyway. Anselm stated that the bodies of the elect in heaven will be perfect, irrespective of what their condition was in life: "there shall be none blind, lame or defective", and only those physical imperfections remain, such as the scars inflicted on martyred saints, which were sustained in pursuit of a righteous life, namely "such defects shall remain as would redound to the glory of the elect", though in general everyone in heaven will be healthy,

---

1. On the theme of perfect bodies after the resurrection see H. J. Weber, *Die Lehre von der Auferstehung der Toten in den Haupttraktaten der scholastischen Theologie von Alexander von Hales zu Duns Skotus* (Freiburger Theologische Studien) (Freiburg: Herder, 1973).

and will suffer "no pain, discomfort or unease" (qtd. in Hughes 1968, 109). These ideas found their way into the Middle High German encyclopedic text called *Lucidarius*, which posed the question what would happen to a person who was eaten by a wolf, which in turn was eaten by a bear, and that by a lion, how could from all that a person be resurrected? The answer was that that which was human flesh was resurrected, and that which was animal stayed dead, since he who had created it can differentiate well between the two. Like a potter who creates a new vessel out of broken shards, so does God create again a beautiful human being who has no impairments.[2] A number of medieval images in manuscripts and wall-paintings in churches depict the idea that wild beasts would dutifully regurgitate and return the scavenged body parts, such as arms and legs, to their rightful owners on the day of the Resurrection. Such imagery includes, for example, the panel paintings of animals bringing together missing body parts from S. Maria di Campo Marzo, Rome, probably made around 1061-1071, and now housed in the Vatican Museum; the mosaic of animals regurgitating those human remains they had scavenged depicted on the west wall of Torcello Cathedral, Venice, dated to the twelfth century; and various manuscript illuminations of an angel ordering body parts to re-assemble, such as in the Trier Apocalypse[3] (from the Ottonian period, the tenth century), or an angel present at the

---

2. A modern German translation of the text in *Lucidarius* reads: "Angenommen, ein Wolf frisst einen Menschen, und den Wolf ein Bär, und den Bären ein Löwe, wie kann aus denen allen der Mensch auferstehen? – Was Menschenfleisch war, das ersteht auf, was dem Tier angehörte, das bleibt [tot]. Der es geschaffen hat, der kann es wohl unterscheiden. Sie erstehen alle so auf, dass ihnen kein Haar fehlt […] Wie ein Hafner, der aus zerbrochenem Ton ein neues Gefäß schafft, so tut Gott: er macht wieder einen schönen Menschen, dem es an nichts gebricht" (Dinzelbacher 2003, 57).
3. Trier, Stadtbibliothek, HS. 31, fol. 67r.

graves opening with missing body parts returned to the cadavers in a manuscript of c.1255 from Bamberg[4] (or Eichstätt). Also in the twelfth century, Peter Lombard used the imagery of a statue being melted down and then reforged out of the same material to explain his view that the resurrected body is basically the same body but remade perfectly; physical defects, therefore, are eliminated at the resurrection (cf. Bynum 1995, 123-4).[5] Such ideas stand in direct opposition to the Egyptian (and Númenórean) beliefs in the *necessity* of *artificially* having to embalm a body to ensure its preservation, since if the promised resurrection is complete and total, what happens to the physical remains in this world become, metaphysically speaking, immaterial and inconsequential.

6 - Discussion

Both mortals (Men, Dwarves) and immortals (Elves) are depicted in Tolkien's legendarium as almost obsessively contemplating the bounds of time and their place within it. Time by definition is something that is fluent, changeable and ephemeral. It was not the simple existence of time that was problematic for both mortal Men and Dwarves and immortal Elves, but this aspect of the flux of time.

> For mortals, the passage of time constantly reminds them of their mortality that, for whatever reason, troubles them. In many ways, this fear of passing time and of mortality is what drives the civilization of Númenor into destruction in the service of Sauron, for example. (Steed 2022, 33)

---

4. Now Stiftsbibliothek Melk, Austria, MS1903 (olim 1833), fol. 109v.
5. Peter Lombard, *Sentences*, Book 4, distinction 44, chapters 1-3.

For the immortals like Elves, the preoccupation with temporality is about slowing down, arresting, practically fossilising the passage of time. The Elves in Middle-earth tried to resist the flow and erosion of time, retreating into their enchanted domains like Lothlórien, where time passed differently from the outside world. Lothlórien embodies the last attempt to achieve any influence over the all too swiftly-flowing river of times, as Frodo observed on the different experience of time within and without Galadriel's realm. On leaving Lothlórien, for example, Frodo and the rest of the company were confused as to how long the Fellowship had been there (*FR*, 'Farewell to Lórien', 370). In his letter of 1954 to Naomi Mitchison, Tolkien said of the Elves:

> with or without his [Sauron's] assistance they were like 'embalmers.' They wanted to have their cake and eat it: to live in the mortal historical Middle-earth because they had become fond of it [...] and to try and stop its change and history, stop its growth, keep it as a pleasaunce, even largely a desert, where they could be 'artists' and they were overburdened with sadness and nostalgic regret. (*Letters*, Letter 154, 197)

But all created things are subject to time, being as they are in the sublunar plane of medieval Christian natural philosophy and astronomy, so this is problematic for Tolkien the Catholic. Hence "in resisting that flow the elves display an unwillingness to accept what the world is and who they are, thereby causing great harm" (Steed 2022, 33). In their pursuit of *stasis*, unchanging longevity, the Elves are harking back to the Two Trees of Valinor as life-preserving gifts to the world; their light bringing vitalism to Arda. It is noteworthy, therefore, to briefly consider a real-world legendary example of life-enhancing trees: the Trees of the Sun and the Moon of medieval fable. Bernard Mandeville's *Travels* (the fourteenth-century equivalent of a bestseller) mentions the Trees of the Sun and the Moon which spoke to Alexander the Great and foretold his death, and are also associated with the legend of Prester John, who, along with unspecified others, is said to guard these trees, eating their fruit and the balm which grows upon them, and thereby living to four or five hundred years (Mandeville 1983, 181). Tolkien's Two Trees primarily give light rather than eternal life, but nonetheless their destruction by Morgoth and Ungoliant also brings death and mortality to the previously immortal realm. As Garth has pointed out, the medieval literary figure of Alexander looking for the earthly paradise in pursuit of immortality is echoed in Tolkien's works by the Númenórean king Ar-Pharazôn the Golden's attack on Valinor, encouraged by the exhortations of an evil vizier-like Sauron (2020, 41).

This paper has explored the two contrasting approaches to the bodies of the dead in Egypt and the Middle Ages, comparing them with the diverse strands of necrological narrative in Tolkien's description of Númenor. The pagan, pre-Christian obsession with corporeal preservation as found in Egyptian practice stands in contrast to the medieval contempt for mortal flesh, since the resurrection would 'correct' any defects or deficits, thereby reducing the importance of physicality. Any interference in the natural order of things should by rights come from divinity alone, since miracle and metaphysics are the domain of God and not of Man. Artifice is what sets apart the Egyptians and Númenóreans, with their obsession about preserving as if alive that which is dead, from medieval Christians, who leave any such preservation to nature, or to God miraculously acting upon nature. The implicit sin is then not so much a sin of wanting everlasting life as such, but of hankering after immortality by using artifice and going against nature. One major character in Tolkien's works exemplified the dangers of artifice only too well. That is Saruman, with his attempts at sub-creation by breeding the Uruk-hai, as well as his love of machines and technology which, by definition, are artifice as opposed to nature. As a Catholic, Tolkien was of course imbued with such Christian ideals, which wove their way into the story of a declining and corrupted Númenórean civilisation, where the ever-greater pursuit of corporeal immortality paralleled an ever-steeper moral decline.

Bibliography

Angenendt, Arnold, '"In meinem Fleisch werde ich Gott sehen." Bernward und die Reliquien', in exhibition catalogue, *Bernward von Hildesheim und das Zeitalter der Ottonen*, ed. by Michael Brandt and Arne Eggebrecht (Hildesheim: Philipp von Zabern, 1993).

Anon., *The Bible, Authorized Version*, (London: The British & Foreign Bible Society, 1954).

Bynum, Caroline Walker, *The Resurrection of the Body in Western Christianity, 200-1336*, (New York: Columbia University Press, 1995).

Camporesi, Piero, *The Incorruptible Flesh: Bodily mutation and mortification in religion and folklore*, trans. by T. Croft-Murray (Cambridge: Cambridge University Press, 1988).

Dinzelbacher, Peter, *Europa im Hochmittelalter 1050-1250. Eine Kultur- und Mentalitätsgeschichte*, (Darmstadt: Primus Verlag, 2003).

Edwards, William, *A Medieval Scrap-Heap*, (London: Rivingtons, 1930).

Ejsmond, Wojciech, 'Natural Pyramids of Ancient Egypt: From emulations of monarchs to royal burials', *Ägypten und Levante/Egypt and the Levant*, 28 (2018), pp. 169-180.

Garth, John, *The Worlds of J.R.R. Tolkien: The Places that Inspired Middle-earth*, (London: Frances Lincoln, 2020).

Hammond, Wayne G., and Christina Scull, *The Lord of the Rings: A Reader's Companion*, (London: HarperCollins, 2005).

Hughes, Robert, *Heaven and Hell in Western Art*, (London: Weidenfeld & Nicolson, 1968).

Mandeville, John, *The Travels of Sir John Mandeville*, trans. by C.W.R.D. Moseley (London: Penguin Books, 1983).

Metzler, Irina, *Disability in Medieval Europe: Thinking about physical impairment during the High Middle Ages, c.1100-1400*, (London: Routledge, 2006).

Reynolds, Pat, 'Death and funerary practices in Middle-earth'. Available at: <https://www.tolkiensociety.org/app/uploads/2016/11/Death-and-funerary-practices-in-Middle-earth.pdf> [accessed 13 August 2023]

Smith, Murray, 'The Wonderful Things of Tutankhamen, Thorin II and Bard', *Amon Hen*, 252 (2015), pp. 2-4.

Steed, Robert, 'This Ephemeral Beauty: Tolkien's Legendarium Through Japanese Buddhist Aesthetic Categories', *Mallorn*, 63 (Winter 2022), pp. 32-34.

Tolkien, J.R.R., *The Silmarillion*, ed. Christopher Tolkien (London: George Allen & Unwin, 1977).
— *Unfinished Tales of Númenor and Middle-earth*, ed. Christopher Tolkien (London: George Allen & Unwin, 1980).
— *The Lord of the Rings,* (London: HarperCollins, 2004).
— *The Letters of J.R.R. Tolkien*, ed. Humphrey Carpenter with the assistance of Christopher Tolkien (London: HarperCollins, 2006).
— *The Nature of Middle-earth*, ed. Carl F. Hostetter (London: HarperCollins, 2021).
— *The Fall of Númenor and Other Tales from the Second Age of Middle-earth*, ed. Brian Sibley (London: Harper Collins, 2022).

"I often dream of it": Trauma and memory in the legacy of the Downfall of Númenor[1]

S.R. Westvik

1 - Introduction

This paper marks the initial forays into a holistic analysis of how trauma responses may be said to be identifiable—to varying degrees—within Tolkien's legendarium outside of the Third Age, evaluating both current clinical diagnostic criteria as well as idiomatic representations of trauma in fiction and testimony. Much has been written about resonances of Tolkien's primary world experiences of trench warfare during the First World War, both in the context of his own life and in its applicability to his fiction, for example in the essential volume *"Something Has Gone Crack": New Perspectives on J.R.R. Tolkien in the Great War* (ed. by Brennan Croft and Röttinger 2019). My objective is to apply to the Númenórean experience an appraisal of both clinical and qualitative historical and critical literature pertaining to trauma, trauma responses, and memory studies informed by my work studying war trauma in witness testimony. The witness authenticity given to the experience of the Second Age's protagonists via the texts' frame narrative resonates strongly with this method. This paper will thus unpack aspects of trauma and memory in understanding the

---

[1]. Content warnings: acute and chronic psychological distress, suicidal ideation.

position of Númenor as a historic tale of legendary importance that has sunk its claws into Middle-earth's hide, precisely because of the enduring awe and terror of its traumatic end. From a wider lens, it will also demonstrate the value of holistic appraisals of trauma symptomatology when accessing witness testimony—whether this witness is in the primary or secondary world—particularly with regards to the roles of narrativisation and literary language in allowing for personal and public processing of traumatic events.

2 - Trauma and Post-Traumatic Stress in the Primary World

To understand the resonances in specific observable behaviours in the texts concerning the Second Age, it serves to highlight both historical and current clinical symptomatology, data, and trends to better understand the benefits in identifying traits as well as the limitations in applying these to cases across cultures and time periods. This appraises the experience as well as the fact of the trauma.

2.1 - Existing clinical frames of diagnosis

There are three core components at the heart of trauma, the first being the instance of the traumatic event itself. The World Health Organisation's ICD-11(International Classification of Diseases), in its entry for "Acute stress reaction", defines a traumatic event as an "event or situation (either short- or long-lasting) of an extremely threatening or horrific nature (e.g., natural or human-made disasters, combat, serious accidents, sexual violence, assault)" (2023a). Traumatic experiences can leave a person "rendered helpless by overwhelming force" that supersedes "ordinary systems of care that give a person a sense of control, connection, and meaning" (Herman 2015). This can in turn result in the development of disorders including anxiety, depression, and PTSD. The second component of trauma is positioning—whether the subject is a direct victim, for example, of a violent attack, or an immediate bystander to say a car crash, or watching a war play out in their home country via television while living overseas. Degrees of separation can impact how a traumatic event is experienced and processed. The final layer is the effect the event experience has on an individual, triggering either acute or chronic trauma responses contextualised with other factors and comorbidities.

Within the ICD-11 symptomatology, an acute stress reaction may include "autonomic signs of anxiety [...] being in a daze, confusion, sadness, anxiety, anger, despair, overactivity, inactivity, social withdrawal, or stupor" (World Health Organisation 2023a). When the individual is removed or reprieved from the event, these reactions subside immediately or within days. When the person's quality of life is adversely impacted over a longer time period, a diagnosis of acute (lasting up to three months) or chronic (lasting longer than 3 months) PTSD may be diagnosed with criteria including the re-experiencing of events through flashbacks, intrusive thoughts or nightmares, avoidance of situations or activities reminiscent of events, or hypervigilance (World Health Organisation 2023b). The memory of the event may be warped or blocked out. Due to or in tandem with this, a breakdown of relationships, self-blame for actions related to or surrounding the traumatic event, survivor's guilt, or attempts to rationalise the violent event may also take place. In a PTSD case, there is significant comorbidity with depression, substance misuse, and premature mortality, for example via suicide.

Most traumatic stressors, it should be noted, do not lead to chronic PTSD. The WHO Mental Health Surveys found that while experiencing trauma and subsequent acute stress reactions is common, the most persistent symptoms of PTSD are highlighted mainly in specific traumatic incidences, the most prevalent being combat experience and sexual violence (Koenen et al. 2017, 2261). Furthermore, trauma can also result in more positive outcomes such as a new or renewed sense of purpose, a phenomenon referred to as post-traumatic growth; resilience has indeed been observed to be a more common response in the wake of trauma compared to PTSD (2261).

There are limitations in the diagnostic evidence base due to interpretation and management of symptoms, particularly as affected by cultural variation. This has given rise to idioms of distress that are not encapsulated by the ICD-11 diagnostic criteria. "Idioms of distress" is a term "[i]nitially used to describe distress in non-western cultures" and based on "ethnographic fieldwork to study socio-cultural context and coping strategies" (Jacob 2019, 7). For example, PTSD cannot sufficiently describe the conditions experienced by the population of Afghanistan over the past decades, where traumatic stress is simultaneously historic *and* ongoing, and where there exists a rich vocabulary of expressions of trauma dictated by prevailing sociocultural and religious norms. The word *churti* ("thinking a lot"), for example, is associated with somatic symptoms of a tight chest and headache (Ventevogel and Faiz 2018, 211). These idioms do not by default indicate the presence of PTSD, but they may point to or intersect with clinically diagnosed symptoms and/or comorbidities, and thus should be interpreted in context to better understand gaps in communication.

It is the awareness of the above limitations that generates an argument for reading trauma in the legendarium within the language and internal experience of the texts, rather than solely imposing a set symptomology on them. This more convincingly and holistically unearths resonances of trauma and PTSD, and is made more effective by examining how these idioms of distress intersect with two themes essential to understanding trauma through the frame narrative of the legendarium: witness testimony and narrativisation.

2.2 - Witness testimony and narrativisation

Observing Tolkien's frame narrative of the legendarium as in-universe texts filtered through his pen, we can treat key Second Age texts somewhat as primary source analysis of witness testimony. Yuval Noah Harari's description of the memoir as a text "dealing with a long time span […] 'written retrospectively'" and where "crucially, 'the author appears as protagonist'" resonates with the 'Akallabêth' (quoted in Bourke 2018, 279). 'Akallabêth', authored by Elendil, stands as history, but simultaneously bears some qualities of memoir as remembered history with qualitative witness observations; one may liken this to Ptolemy's lost firsthand accounts of Alexander the Great's campaigns (*UT*, Loc. 4701[2]). By comparison, 'The Disaster of the Gladden Fields' has additional degrees of separation; it may be viewed similarly to the filtering of Ptolemy's accounts through Arrian's *Anabasis*, a historical text informed by contemporary witness sources inaccessible to the reader.

Taking memory in hand allows us to then understand how the field of memory studies has moved towards understanding

---

[2]. Due to lack of page numbers on Kindle devices, the location or "loc" numeral is provided for eBooks cited in this paper. The "loc" numeral corresponds to the relevant string of text in the eBook and is fixed regardless of adjustment to changes in font or page size.

memory as a fluid and imaginative process. Research finds that remembered experiences, particularly as written into text, are characterised by fluidity and silences that are "built into them" (Winter 2018, 27), which testify to idioms of distress as much as to clinical symptoms of "fragmented" flashbacks, memory lapses, or changes (Bellot 2020, 20). Because traumatic events are themselves lapses in the natural order of things, "the imaginative quality of literary narrative allows it to access the traumatic experience and gesture towards or evoke trauma" (Pederson 2018, 99). It also fulfils the need for narrative constructions to create coherence following trauma (Dwyer 2018, 7). Given Tolkien was himself a First World War veteran, the legendarium is a unique literary vehicle to examine resonances of trauma through the lens of secondary world witnesses as flowing from the pen of the author as a primary world witness to traumatic events, however unintentional or intentional any resonances to those events may be. It should be noted that it is not the goal of this paper to look into intentionality.

Returning to 'The Disaster of the Gladden Fields', we do not know the author(s), but we do know that it is based on firsthand witness testimony from two individuals: Isildur's squire Ohtar, referred to by his rank rather than his name; and Estelmo, the squire of Elendur, Isildur's firstborn. Others on the scene were Woodmen living in the eaves of the Greenwood and Elves dispatched by Thranduil. All accounts were further filtered and informed by evidence obtained during the Fourth Age under Aragorn II's reign and by the in-universe author(s) of 'The Disaster of the Gladden Fields', and the story is referred to as "surmise: but well-founded" and as a "legend" (*UT*, Loc. 5705). While a function of the pseudo-historical nature of the text, this does still provide an interesting frame by which to understand trauma because it allows for the aforementioned gaps and ambiguities, which are couched in deeply emotive and personal language. Thus, while framed as a historical text, the manner of its telling demonstrates an inclination towards Pederson's observation that the "historical objective of archival language fails to capture traumatic experience" (2018, 98).

"Idioms of distress", as discussed above, elegantly encapsulates a concept that can be adjusted in its usage to gesture towards word choices, silences, and gaps in communication when processing and expressing the traumatic experiences of individuals or communities. Idiom itself carries aspects of shared narrative, springing from history, turns of phrase, cultural reference points, and fables. Nevertheless, trauma is experienced on two levels that impact how it is conveyed. The interior individual experience, by its nature, cannot be accurately imparted for it is inaccessible to any objective metric, it can only be suggested, by allusion or context. This is amplified on the national level where objective realities of a traumatic event may be shared, but subjective experiences are still confined to each person or filtered through a subgroup of peoples and must be in discourse with factual events. Therefore, we must acknowledge that language, too, has confines, and "proves insufficient to express the horror of […] violence, terror" (Bellot 2020, 19). Generational and linguistic differences can also affect the gaps in the social fabric through which a contemporary observer might glimpse trauma, as well as the way in which the trauma may be transformed by narrative.

3 - Interpreting witness testimony in the Secondary World

In the following analysis I will apply some of these aspects of witness testimony to the experiences of Elendil, Isildur, and very briefly touch on the Third Age to speak to the enduring nature of trauma in national memory.

3.1 - Númenor and collective trauma

Númenor is a people, a history, and a culture steeped in memory—a thing individuated yet "also about the community, the collective, and the nation" and thus existing "in a symbiotic relationship with the public memorialisation of the past" , where the self and one's place in the world is in part sculpted by the articulation of memory in a social, intergenerationally transmissible way (Abrams 2010, 54). The great hallmark of Númenórean identity is that of being both persons and a nation in exile. Exile is traumatic, through the events that precipitated displacement, the process, and the aftermath. 'Akallabêth' is a harrowing narrative of person-to-person violence, natural disaster, and forced migration. From research done about children in Sri Lanka in the wake of civil conflict that occurred at the same time as the 2004 tsunami in the Indian ocean, we know that the combination of traumatic manmade and natural events can lead to a prevalence of chronic disorders including PTSD (Soysa 2013). With this in mind, we can understand why expressions of trauma in the survivors often translated to yearning felt for their lost homeland and forms of memorialisation in witness-penned national histories and monuments.

Over decades of a widening sociopolitical rift, and three years of Sauron's manipulation of Ar-Pharazôn and eventual overwhelming radicalisation of the island, the conditions for chronic stress reactions were cultured due to sustained incidences of stress. In 'Akallabêth' Tolkien writes of how "madness and sickness assailed [Númenóreans]…[a]nd men took weapons in those days and slew one another for little cause", as well as the Faithful being specifically victimised by the King's Men under Sauron's leadership—a state of affairs that generates chronic fear, stress, and paranoia for the persecuted minority (*Silmarillion*, Loc. 5069). This is the same way PTSD can develop in a warzone through heightened stress over numerous weeks or months. The caveat does remain that to this day, research is still inconclusive as to what other vulnerabilities may make certain people more likely to develop PTSD in these situations.

At this point, it is important to recall that this depiction of Númenor comes from the pen of Elendil; therefore, the traumatic incidents captured here come from a witness, either as a direct participant or one or two degrees removed. We can argue then that in speaking for the collective as well as his personal trauma, Elendil is imposing his responses of not only what he experienced himself but what he saw occurring to other people in his ill-fated country of birth. Using the allowance of literary language to spotlight idioms of distress, the following close reading will evaluate traumatic events in his history and that of his son Isildur.

3.2 - Elendil

As previously described, some of the comorbidities of chronic stress reactions include depression, self-blame, rationalising an act of violence, and suicidal ideation. To varying degrees, we find all of these within Elendil's narrative. The first of course is familial loss. Grief is traumatic, and can be a comorbidity of PTSD or simply acute trauma by itself. When Elendil loses his father Amandil, the latter's words emphasise themes of exile and death. Amandil says that "you should lose all that you have loved, foretasting death in life, seeking a land in exile elsewhere" (*Silmarillion*, Loc. 5111). These themes stay with Elendil as a persistent, harrowing grief. They first return when he journeys "in secret to the western shores and as he gazed out over the sea, sorrow and yearning were upon him, and he greatly loved his father" (Loc. 5123). This yearning chimes with a 1678 observation by Johannes Hofer upon the return of Swiss soldiers fighting abroad. He documented a serious, life-threatening form of homesickness classed as a mental condition or nervous disorder which he dubbed "nostalgia" (quoted in Hron 2018, 288). While this isn't clinically considered a disorder or disease today, resonances of it can be seen in how "migrant groups have been linked to higher incidences of diseases including depression", a comorbidity of chronic stress response (Hron 2018, 288). This nostalgia sustains itself apparently indefinitely for Elendil individually and the exiled Númenóreans culturally.

A brief diversion is needed here to discuss exile further. As opposed to immigrants or refugees, an "exile evokes notions of guilt or innocence and just or unjust suffering" and is also often characterised by an alienated condition (287). Sayad's "*la double absence*" speaks to how the exiled subject, when writing fiction, "remains physically both in the former home and the new host country as well as the past and the present in an ambiguous state of twin identities" (quoted in Hron 2018, 289-90). This state of mind of constant nostalgia or yearning is evident in the post-Downfallen world. As an individual, Elendil frequently avails of the Emyn Beraid built by his friend Gil-galad, where he ascends to look across the sea in yearning for glimpses of Númenor in a manner that becomes habitual—a chronic behaviour. For the Númenóreans more broadly, "they longed ever to escape from the shadow of their exile to see some fashion of the light that dies not, for the sorrow of the thought of death had pursued them over the deeps of the sea" (*Silmarillion*, Loc. 5215). Mired so deep in this grief, their shared traumatic experiences had pursued them to such a degree that the effects of the memories were no longer acute, and had become a chronic fixture of national memory. Furthermore, the use of the word "shadow" as a visual and emotive cloud is evidenced throughout the legendarium. For example, following the War of the Last Alliance, the text speaks to how "there was in Thranduil's heart a still deeper shadow. He had seen the horror of Mordor and could not forget it. If ever he looked south its memory dimmed the light of the Sun" (*UT*, Loc. 5407). Traumatic events and the language of shadow are thus intrinsically and idiomatically linked across Tolkien's writing

The final aspect to address is suicidal ideation. During the flight of the Faithful ships, the text states "when the devouring wave rolled over the land and Númenor toppled to its fall, then Elendil would have been overwhelmed or would have deemed it the lesser grief to perish, for no wrench of death could be more bitter than the loss and agony of that day" (*Silmarillion*, Loc. 5183). In terms of studies about PTSD both suicidal ideation and attempts are logged as comorbidities to having PTSD, with the latter being unfortunately more quantifiable than the former. This depiction nevertheless resonates powerfully with the symptomology of trauma responses, which sometimes fit into the classic PTSD categorisation, and other times reflect conditions like depression which can be a comorbidity for suicidal ideation.

3.3 - Isildur

With Isildur's storyline during the Downfall, we don't get a sense that he necessarily experiences acute or lasting trauma.

Even when he is assailed during his successful bid to steal the fruit of Nimloth, it's explicitly written that after he was wounded, he later arose and was "troubled no more by his wounds" (*Silmarillion*, Loc. 5054). As we know from examples like Frodo's stab wound from the Witch-king on Amon Sûl or his sting from Shelob, there are cases where wounds can endure and trigger adverse physiological reactions on trauma anniversaries. This tracks with an observable phenomenon of trauma anniversaries triggering physiological responses. In the case of Nimloth, Isildur's wounds do not last, and do not have any evidential impact on his psychological wellbeing in the immediate aftermath.

This changes for Isildur after the War of the Last Alliance more so than 'Akallabêth', however, in a manner that suggests cumulative stress. In the Second Age 3429, Isildur is forced to flee with his children and pregnant wife after Sauron's attack on his new home of Minas Ithil. Shortly after this, he commences active participation in a seven-year military siege against Sauron. During this time, he loses many troops, and finally his father to violent wartime deaths. This prompts Isildur's famous line about claiming the Ring as weregild for his family's deaths (Loc. 5424). It is notable that Tolkien uses a singular sentence to then connect Isildur keeping the Ring with memorialisation: "Taking it therefore he returned at first to Minas Anor and there planted the white tree in memory of his brother Anárion" (Loc. 5424). The Ring together with this sapling from a destroyed home, planted in memory of a lost loved one, become the vehicles by which we understand the traumatic effects of the cumulative years of sustained stress that Isildur endured. The Ring becomes part of how Isildur does or does not process his experiences, as much as his acts of personal and national memory forming, as it is part of his immediate post-war actions to claim and retain ownership of the Ring.

The Ring is a vehicle for inflicting and sustaining pain, that by its nature cannot be mastered by those under its influence, from which it remains extremely difficult to escape, even after being parted from the physical presence of the Ring. There is resonance here with the nature of trauma as a lasting burden that exerts an often unyielding pressure on survivors. Traumatic memory is heavily connected to the body, where physiological symptoms are tied to psychological stress, and the Ring's impact on those other than Sauron who wield it demonstrates similar hallmarks. Isildur describes how the Ring "was hot when I first took it, hot as a glede, so that I doubt if ever again I shall be free of the pain of it", and he also says that "it is precious to me, though I buy it with great pain" (*FR*, 'The Council of Elrond', 252-3). The Ring is thus explicitly tied to pain that cannot be escaped, and to Isildur's post-war experience and responses to grief. He takes it willingly, as one may willingly take on the burden of going into a situation where trauma may form, like a warzone, but that self-command is stripped when it comes to letting the burden go. There is indeed also an important element of seduction in the qualities of the Ring that plays a role in its maintaining a grip on the wearer, but examining the relationship of that with trauma is beyond the current scope of this discussion.

When we get to 'Disaster of the Gladden Fields', a highly traumatic event, the text does not allow much room to examine individuated trauma because of the degrees of separation from witnesses as well as the deaths of all involved except Ohtar, Estelmo, and one other unnamed witness. However, the language used in the telling couches the event in phrases that still emphasise the traumatic impact of the event on the protagonists, and even imagine the trauma faced by them when the narrative goes into what Isildur experiences alone during his flight. None of the in-universe authors could have known what was going through Isildur's mind when he fled alone from the site of the ambush, but it is included as a key part of the narratorial recollection of events as transmitted in the in-universe written history. For example, the account includes an overheard conversation between Elendur and Isildur, reconstructed from Estelmo's firsthand accounts, then goes on to describe that as Isildur fled, "[h]e was in great pain and anguish of heart and he ran like a stag from the hounds", and later felt "lost and alone, a small creature in the wilds of Middle-earth" (*UT*, Loc. 5691). Nobody was there to witness the flight itself, or its outcome. Some of this description must naturally come from narrative interest on Tolkien's part, but combined with the frame narrative it nevertheless shows the importance of qualitative depictions of events in in-universe texts.

Returning briefly to the Ring as a vehicle of trauma, the loss of the Ring in the Anduin gives Isildur a brief respite before his passing, and this is included in the narrative as well. "It left his hand", it is written, and "so overwhelming was his sense of loss he struggled no more, and would have sunk and drowned (Loc. 5691). But swift as it had come the mood passed. The pain had left him. A great burden had been taken away" (Loc. 5691). This has some resonance in the way traumatic burdens can pass through phases of impact upon a person. Frodo, in giving up the Ring, found relief initially, but the enduring trauma returned after his removal from the circumstances of overwhelming stress, particularly on anniversaries, and impacted his later quality of life such that he had to depart Middle-earth entirely to seek healing. Had Isildur lived, we may have seen something similar in him, or perhaps he would have moved towards post-traumatic growth. We will never know due to his tragic passing.

However, one interesting thing of note is found at the conclusion of the core account of 'Disaster of the Gladden Fields', where, after Isildur is slain, it is written, "so passed the first victim of the malice of the masterless Ring, Isildur second king of the Dúnedain, lord of Arnor and Gondor" (Loc. 5691). It is notable that Tolkien chooses to refer to Isildur as a victim. This phrasing emphasises the manner in which the Ring—this encompassing shadowy force of grief and of physical and psychological trauma — can strip away a person's agency. Tolkien's axis of moral failure as described with regards to Frodo, and the increasing physical and psychological torments laid upon him, declares that his ultimate failure in destroying the Ring is one that cannot be judged with any force of malice, but with mercy, because of these pressures (*Letters*, Letter 246, 460-1). The thesis stands that the greater and more numerous the external traumatic pressures, the less moral failure can be said to apply to an individual's actions, even if the action itself is a failure. It is a subtle thematic statement of great compassion on Tolkien's part and a revealing aspect of the event's appraisal by the text's in-universe historians, who close out the depiction of the disaster with notes of tragedy and pity, not blame.

One can then collate Isildur's initial experiences during the Downfall—sustained social stress, physical hurt, and survival of a natural disaster, with no observable initial traumatic effect—and add to this the cumulative effects of invasion, forced evacuation, seven years of sustained martial stress in an entrenched position in the inhospitable domain of Mordor, and great personal loss, which do have observable psychological and social effects of grief and lasting pain. With these factors appraised together, Tolkien's choice to describe Isildur as a victim of the Ring gains great depth and can be viewed as being determined by a similar axis upon which Frodo's actions were judged. Along with the rest of the text of 'Disaster of the Gladden Fields', the great pain and torment that Isildur experienced becomes intrinsic to the narrativisation of the event itself. It is a narrative that paints him as somebody with the common human foible of pride, but who nevertheless carries the burdens of past traumatic events and is ultimately characterised as a victim of the power of the Ring. The Second Age texts concerning Isildur are thus texts not dedicated solely to fact-finding or analysis. Gesturing towards trauma is essential to remembering, narrativising, and historicising the events at the Gladden Fields to the history's authors within the legendarium's frame narrative, just as it is to remembering the Downfall of Númenor.

3.4 - The Third Age

This paper would be incomplete without presenting a few short notes regarding the Third Age. Here, the notion of witness gains a new dimension as the speakers and writers of history move past the time of living, mortal witness memory. Naturally, immortals exist within Middle-earth, so Elrond, for example, has witness memory to history that contributes to some texts, such as his recollections of Elendur's appearance (*UT*, Loc. 5884). However, for those people who retain these stories as part of their national narrative—the successors of Gondor and Arnor and the latter's eventual fragmented domains—these events would not have been known in living memory beyond two or three generations. It is similar, for example, to the manner in which individuals born in the late 1990s and early 2000s are, for the most part, the last generation to have spoken to witnesses of the Second World War. The generation born in the 2010s will have largely heard about these events second hand from the custodians of witness memory (e.g. children and grandchildren of survivors), recordings, films, or books, as the generation of contemporaneous witnesses dies out. The degrees of separation from lived experience will only increase, as is already the case for the First World War, for example, turning memory to story and legend even more than current cultural memory has already done.

In a similar way, proximity as witnesses and to witnesses is lost for the descendants of Gondor and Arnor who own these stories as national memory, even as the stories endure through to the beginning of the Fourth Age. They form the backbone of actions taken and arguments built during the War of the Ring, a key example being the importance of the entire chapter 'The Council of Elrond'. We also see that these events still resonate very strongly down generational lines through Faramir's recurring dream of the wave that devoured Númenor (*RK*, 'The Steward and the King', 962). John Rosegrant argues that Tolkien's "Atlantis-haunted" dreams, which in turn inspired Faramir's dream, were in many ways traumatic dreams in and of themselves (2019, 100). One may therefore assert that the Fall of Númenor, in being born of this dream, has trauma woven directly into its collapsed bedrock from its primary world beginning through its secondary world formation and depiction, and as such trauma is woven into the memory of trees and stone as much as into the stories, songs, dreams, and the very DNA of Númenor's living descendants.

4 - Conclusion

The next steps in this research are to explore additional cases studies appraising trauma responses following natural disasters, to better account for the effects of the Downfall upon survivors, as well as to look more deeply into post-traumatic growth. There is further room to expand on idioms of distress, particularly the use of "shadow", as well as other traumatised groups in the legendarium. For now, this paper will satisfy itself as having been an overview of how our present understanding of trauma, stress responses, PTSD, and other disorders can resonate powerfully with fictional texts. This is in part because of the nature of taking a literary, idiomatic approach to describing trauma, which generates the gaps and silences that allow Tolkien to gesture towards the internalised, subjective experiences of traumatic events. It is also because the frame narrative, with its sculpting of the Second Age texts as pseudo-historical witness accounts, explicitly depicts personal and collective traumatic experiences as integral to social and national recollection of traumatic events.

Bibliography

Abrams, Lynn, *Oral History Theory*, (Oxon: Routledge, 2010).

Bellot, A.R., 'Authoring War Memories: War Memoir Writing and Testimonial Theatre Performances', *Analyses/Rereadings/Theories: A Journal Devoted to Literature, Film and Theatre*, 6.1 (2020), pp. 18-27.

Bourke, Joanna, 'Pugnacity, Pain and Professionalism: British Combat Memoirs from Afghanistan, 2006-14', in *War Stories: The War Memoir in History and Literature*, ed. by Philip Dwyer (New York: Berghahn Books, 2018), pp. 277-300.

Dwyer, Philip, 'Making Sense of the Muddle', in *War Stories: The War Memoir in History and Literature*, ed. by Philip Dwyer (New York: Berghahn Books, 2018), pp. 1-26.

Herman, Judith, *Trauma and Recovery: The Aftermath of Violence–From Domestic Abuse to Political Terror*, (New York: Basic Books, 2022).

Hron, Madelaine, 'The Trauma of Displacement', in *Trauma and Literature*, ed. by J. Roger Kurtz (Cambridge: Cambridge University Press, 2018), pp. 284-298.

Jacob, K. S., 'Idioms of distress, mental symptoms, syndromes, disorders and transdiagnostic approaches', *Asian Journal of Psychiatry*, 46 (2019), p. 7.

Koenen, K. C., A. Ratanatharathorn, L. Ng, K. A. McLaughlin, E. J. Bromet, D. J. Stein, and others, 'Posttraumatic Stress Disorder in the World Mental Health Surveys', *Psychological Medicine*, 47 (2017), pp. 2260–2274.

Pederson, Joshua, 'Trauma and Narrative', in *Trauma and Literature*, ed. by J. Roger Kurtz, (Cambridge: Cambridge University Press 2018), pp. 97-109.

Rosegrant, John, 'Fault Lines Beneath the Crack', in *"Something Has Gone Crack": New Perspectives on J.R.R. Tolkien in the Great War*, ed. by Janet Brennan Croft and Annika Röttinger (Zurich: Walking Tree Press 2019), pp. 95-120.

Soysa, Champika K., 'War and Tsunami PTSD Responses in Sri Lankan Children: Primacy of Reexperiencing and Arousal Compared to Avoidance-

Numbing', *Journal of Aggression, Maltreatment & Trauma*, 22.8 (2013), pp. 896–915.

Tolkien, J.R.R., *Unfinished Tales of Númenor and Middle-earth*, ed. by Christopher Tolkien (London: HarperCollins, 2009). Kindle edition.
— *The Silmarillion*, ed. by Christopher Tolkien (London: HarperCollins, 2011). Kindle edition.
— *The Lord of the Rings*, (London: HarperCollins, 2022). Kindle edition.
— *The Letters of J.R.R. Tolkien: Revised and Expanded Edition*, ed. by Humphrey Carpenter with the assistance ofChristopher Tolkien (London: HarperCollins, 2023).

Ventevogel, Peter and Faiz, Hafizullah, 'Mental disorder or emotional distress? How psychiatric surveys in Afghanistan ignore the role of gender, culture and context', *Intervention*, 16.3 (2018), p. 211.

Winter, Jay, 'War memoirs, Witnessing and Silence', in *War Stories: The War Memoir in History and Literature*, ed. by Philip Dwyer (New York: Berghahn Books, 2018), pp. 27-39.

World Health Organization, *QE84 Acute stress reaction*, database entry, ICD-11, January 2023a, <https://icd.who.int/browse11/l-m/en#/http%3A%2F%2Fid.who.int%2Ficd%2Fentity%2F505909942> [accessed 14 August 2023].

World Health Organization, *6B40 Post traumatic stress disorder*, database entry, ICD-11, January 2023b <https://icd.who.int/browse11/l-m/en#/http%3A%2F%2Fid.who.int%2Ficd%2Fentity%2F2070699808> [accessed 14 August 2023].

"Foretasting Death in Life": Desire, the Fall, and Attempting to Return the 'Gift' of Ilúvatar

Sara Brown

J.R.R. Tolkien's Atlantean myth of Númenor traces the story of the rise and fall of one of the greatest civilisations of the Middle-earth legendarium. Despite the gift of a lifespan far beyond that of other mortal Men, an increasing anxiety of death combined with illimitable belief in their own superiority leads inexorably to rebellion against the Valar, and hence to utter destruction.

That Tolkien chose to refer to death as a 'gift' reveals his own ideas on the nature of mortality and the possibility of an 'afterlife.' Through the story of Númenor, Tolkien appears to be exploring a potential outcome for the rejection of that gift; however, it is evident that it is not simply the Númenóreans' fear of death that leads to their downfall; hubris and the desire for power and possessions also play a role as colonialism, slavery, and the seizure of natural resources for personal enrichment are additional indicators of a fall from grace. What is clear is that a moral judgment on these actions is made, by Ilúvatar but also through the actions and decisions of the author, and punishment is thus meted out accordingly. However, it should also be noted that Tolkien himself employed ambiguity in his use of words such as 'death;' as Claudio Testi notes, 'death' in Tolkien's works can sometimes mean a "separation of soul and body," and at other times mean the "departure of the soul from the Circles of the World" (2012, 49). 'Immortality' is also a contested term; Tolkien occasionally used the word to describe the Elves, such as in Letter 131 to Milton Waldman, where he explains that:

> The Elves are 'immortal,' at least as far as this world goes: and hence are concerned rather with the griefs and burdens of deathlessness in time and change, than with death. (*Letters*, Letter 131, 205)

He also employs the words 'immortal' and 'immortality' elsewhere in his writing (see, for example, *Shaping*, 100; *Silmarillion,* 114, 262), although often with some small caveat, such as "as far as this world goes" as seen in the letter above.

It is worth noting, though, that Tolkien also remarks in other places that this is not actually the correct word to use, for example in *Morgoth's Ring* (331), and also Letter 156 to Father Robert Murray, where he explains that:

> the point of view of this mythology is that 'mortality' or a short span, and 'immortality' or an indefinite span was part of what we might call the biological and spiritual *nature* of the Children of God, Men and Elves (the firstborn) respectively, and could *not* be altered by anyone (even a Power or god), and would not be altered by the One, except perhaps by one of those strange exceptions to all rules and ordinances which seem to crop up in the history of the Universe. (*Letters*, Letter 156, 300)

Instead, we are told of the Elves' 'serial longevity'[1] which, as I will explain later, may not be as desirable a state as the later Númenóreans perceived and believed it to be. I would argue, though, that there may be an explanation for the differences between Letter 131 and Letter 156, namely that Letter 156 is written to a Jesuit priest who would have had both a greater knowledge and deeper understanding of the spiritual issues that are raised by 'immortality' versus 'serial longevity;' Tolkien may not have felt that the explanation he offers Fr Robert Murray to have been either useful or necessary to Milton Waldman.

Semantics aside, the later Númenóreans became bitterly envious of what they believed the Elves enjoyed: a limitless lifespan in which to enjoy the world and all it has to offer, and rejected the idea that a mortal life, with its inevitable end and the mystery of that end, could be a 'gift.' The first question is why Tolkien presents death as a gift, as this might initially seem counterintuitive. Indeed, this is the "strange gift of Ilúvatar," who willed "that the hearts of Men should seek beyond this world and should find no rest therein; but they should have a virtue to shape their life, amid the powers of the world, beyond the Music of the Ainur, which is as fate to all things else" (*Silmarillion*, 41). This gift is further referred to as a "gift of freedom" as, unlike the Elves, "the children of Men dwell only a short space in the world alive, and are not bound to it, and depart soon whither the Elves know not" (42). What happens to the Atani therefore remains a mystery, one that even the Elves found troubling, referring to it as the "Doom of Men" (265). The Elven messengers who go to Númenor to respond to their claim that Elven immortality is to be envied by the mortal races, can only reply by saying:

---

[1]. See, for example, *Letters* 385, 405; *Morgoth* 331; *OFS* 68.

> Indeed the mind of Ilúvatar concerning you is not known to the Valar, and he has not revealed all things that are to come. But this we hold to be true, that your home is not here, neither in the Land of Aman nor anywhere within the Circles of the World. (265)

As Christopher Garbowski remarks, "Trust is paramount in the 'gift.' Tolkien gives a less conventional (but nonetheless orthodox) reading of Genesis in that the Fall is not the cause of death, which was already present before the Fall; the Fall is rather the inability to accept death - which can be understood as a lack of trust in God. This not only refers to a single moment of our history, but is constantly repeated, for instance, in the story of the downfall of Númenor" (1997, 31). In 'Laws and Customs of the Eldar,' Manwë reminds us that this trust is founded on the belief that Ilúvatar "is good, and that his works shall all end in good" (*Morgoth*, 245). The Númenóreans begin with that trust but, over the centuries, this erodes until the gift is regarded only with suspicion and bitterness.

Tolkien's belief in the gift of death was rooted in his Catholic faith, which held that death was a natural part of the human condition and that, although a kind of ending, it offered the possibility of eternal life. Tolkien saw death not as an end, but as a doorway to a new and greater existence, one in which individuals could be reunited with loved ones and experience the ultimate fulfilment of their hopes and dreams. As Tom Shippey suggests, "The Silmarillion [...] seems to be trying to persuade us to see death as potentially a gift or reward. [...] [Moreover,] the elvishness of the elves is meant to reflect back on the humanity of man" (1992, 210-1). This 'elvishness' to which Shippey is referring is this perceived immortality that the Númenóreans believe the Elves to enjoy;

however, it is apparent that they do not fully understand what this 'immortality' truly means, and here is where we may begin to understand the way in which death may, in fact, be a gift.

The Elves are bound to Middle-earth in a way that the mortal races are not. They are immune from disease, can recover from wounds that would otherwise be fatal, and will reincarnate if their body, the *hröa*, is slain, but they cannot break out of this cycle of life and death. Like the Valar, they are tied to Arda until its ultimate end, which is a moment beyond the capability of even the Valar to foresee; this binding has the added effect that Elves change and age in different ways to mortal beings: Elves do not age in the visible and physical way that Men do, but they become weary, burdened by the sorrows of the world, and doomed to fade into a wraith-like state as their *feä* is consumed by their *hröa* unless they travel west to Aman. Their fate after the ending of Arda is just as unknown as the fate of Men after death; some form of 'death,' as mortals understand it, therefore seems certain but may well be regarded by the Elves as a blessed escape from the trials of extended life. Elvish serial longevity, and their inevitable consequent fading, demonstrates the shortcomings of Deathlessness: immortality and being tied to the world is not necessarily enviable. However, this very 'elvishness of the Elves,' as Shippey puts it, is what leads mortal beings who live alongside them in the same world to question the nature of the gift of Ilúvatar, and the mystery of what lies beyond. Humans are famously uncomfortable with mystery, especially something as significant as the question of what happens after death.

This resonates with what we read in the 'Athrabeth Finrod ah Andreth,' where Tolkien tells us that "even the Wise among us have given too little thought to Arda itself, or to other things that dwell here. We have thought most of ourselves; of how our hröar and fëar should have dwelt together for ever in joy, and of the darkness impenetrable that now awaits us" (*Morgoth*, 318). As Garbowski comments,

> For Andreth, death is both the swift hunter and 'impenetrable' darkness. The reality of death proves the dualism of creation. Like classical dualists the wise woman uses the imagery of light and darkness, but whereas the former distinguished the immortal spirit from matter, which they disdained, Andreth sees life as light and death as darkness. (1997, 30)

If life for the mortal races is fleeting, especially in comparison to the serial longevity of the Eldar, then finding meaning in that life must come with trust in the gift of Ilúvatar, otherwise life becomes only the brief period of time before death, and death then has greater meaning and significance than life itself. Here is where we turn to the fate of the Númenóreans in the Second Age, for whom death became increasingly more significant than life and, as a result, this once proud nation stepped onto a path that would eventually lead to utter destruction.

The first Númenóreans were blessed by Ilúvatar with the Land of Gift as a reward for their defiance of Morgoth. The island of Númenor was "raised by Ossë out of the depths of the Great Water, and it was established by Aulë and enriched by Yavanna; and the Eldar brought thither flowers and fountains out of Tol Eressëa" (*Silmarillion*, 312). The people themselves were stronger, taller – Elendil was said to have been almost eight feet tall – wiser, and longer-lived than other Atani (*UT*, 304). The one rule they had to abide by was not to sail West to seek the Undying Lands. This ban on going to Aman is Manwë's decree and is meant for their protection, so that these ennobled Men do not become "enamoured of the immortality of the Valar and the Eldar and the lands where all things endure" (*Silmarillion*, 315). In return, the island was a place of great beauty and peace for many centuries, and the Númenóreans accepted death as an inevitable part of life that was nothing to fear.

In the Third Age, Aragorn's attitude to death reflects the acceptance of the first Númenóreans of the gift of Ilúvatar. Instead of fighting it, he chooses, as did the first Númenórean kings, the time and manner of his death to avoid waiting until "I wither and fall from my high seat witless and unmanned" (*RK*, 'Appendix A', 1037). Instead, he is grateful that "to me has been given not only a span thrice that of Men of Middle-earth, but also the grace to go at my will, and give back the gift" (1037). What does he mean by "give back the gift"? For Aragorn, death is simply the counterpart to the gift of life, both bestowed upon him by Ilúvatar, and thus not to be feared, but embraced willingly.

Whereas the Kings of Númenor had previously done as Aragorn would later do, always trusting in and willingly accepting the gift of Ilúvatar, this acceptance gradually erodes as it becomes mingled with fear. As trust in the Elves and the Valar wanes, so too does belief in the beneficence of Eru and his assertion that death is, indeed, a gift. The first kings pass the sceptre on in good time, before they are too old to rule well, and this lasts until the twelfth king, Tar-Ciryatan, who forces his father, Tar-Minastir, to hand over the sceptre in SA 1869 and is the first to speak openly against the Ban of the Valar. This is the first sign of things to come, as the reign of Tar-Ciryatan also sees the beginning of the Númenórean policy of oppressing the Men of Middle-earth and exacting heavy tribute, where before there had been friendship and cooperation. The Númenóreans make Umbar into a great fortress in SA 2280 and significantly expand Pelargir, a landing in Gondor near the Mouths of the Anduin, in SA 2350. Tar-Ciryatan's son, Tar-Atanamir, ignores the messengers of Manwë and is known as 'the Unwilling'; he is the first king to refuse to give up his life and sceptre, so "lived to a great age, clinging to life beyond the end of all joy", refusing to accept the gift until it was thrust upon him against his will - a practice that then became the norm as none of his successors relinquished the sceptre prior to death (*Silmarillion*, 266).

The prospect of death, despite their greatly extended lifespan, began to dominate the thoughts and fears of the descendants of Elros. The attitude of the Númenóreans becomes first more interrogative, and then increasingly bitter, as they demand to know why "the Lords of the West sit there in peace unending, while we must die and go we know not whither, leaving our home and all that we have made?" and, later, "Why should we not envy the Valar, or even the least of the Deathless? For of us is required a blind trust, and a hope without assurance, knowing not what lies before us in a little while. And yet we also love the Earth and would not lose it" (264-5). Envy, yes, but also a fear of death and the unknown that is the inevitable result of the erosion of trust in the 'gift' of Ilúvatar.

Númenor falls further under the shadow, and we are told that "the fear of death grew ever darker upon them, and they delayed it by all means that they could" (320). As Kristine Larsen explains: "as time went on, the Númenóreans, especially the rulers, began to resent their mortality and began to question why they were not permitted to sail to the Blessed Lands. The kings began to cling to life, waiting until they were infirm to grudgingly die, and scientists were tasked with trying to discover the secrets of eternal life" (2020, 3). If the prime motivation for mortals is indeed a never-ending and primal search for the meaning in life, then clearly the Númenóreans turn away from this, finding no meaning in life, only in death. This means that they inevitably fail to fully participate in life itself as they concern themselves solely with its inevitable end and, in so doing, become slaves to their fear. Richard Purtill observes that even Sauron himself - can be perceived as a slave of "his own fear and hate" (1984, 57). Instead of putting trust in the gift, Númenóreans are made fearful of death by Morgoth, who has "cast his shadows upon it, and confounded it with darkness, and brought forth evil out of good, and fear out of hope" (*Silmarillion*, 42). Their growing fear of death, which leads them to hatred of the Valar and the Elves, ironically removes their freedom and leaves them bound to their physical bodies as if they were in actual shackles.

Their success in the quest for power and riches further fuelled the hubris of the Númenóreans. Increasing predatory expeditions to the coast of Middle-earth and greater colonisation over the peoples of those lands are the inevitable result of the pride and greed of the later Númenóreans, for whom the Isle of Gift has become too small to contain their desire for the fortunes to be made on those coasts. They strip and mine the natural resources, sometimes trading but often exacting them as tribute. These natural resources also include slaves who, by the final days of Númenor, are often used as human sacrifices in the temple built under Sauron's aegis to honour Morgoth. A tantalising snippet of these days may be found in the incomplete story 'Tal-Elmar', in *The Peoples of Middle-earth*, in which we are told first how the Númenóreans would come feigning friendship, taking the opportunity to "spy out the land and the numbers of the folk, and then go" (*Peoples*, 427). The ships would then return, but this time "it is in other guise [...] they bear away evil booty, captives packed like beasts, the fairest women and children, or young men unblemished, and that is their end" (427). When a fleet of Númenórean vessels anchor off the shore, his fearful tribe send Tal-Elmar to investigate, but the Númenóreans greet him as a long-lost kinsman. At that point, the story breaks off, and no more is told of Tal-Elmar's mysterious origins or his fate.

The motif of imperialism is there from the first drafts of the story of Númenor. In *The Lost Road*, Tolkien writes of the Númenóreans' desire to "conquer new realms for our race, and ease the pressure of this peopled island, where every road is trodden hard, and every tree and grass blade counted. To be free, and masters of the world", suggesting more than a hint of settler colonialism (*Lost Road*, 60). The second Númenor story, no longer directly connected to the primary world, is the fall of Númenor, contemporaneous with *The Lost Road*. Here, Tolkien writes of the Númenórean king Tarkalion, who, believing that the gods had delivered the dominion of the earth to the Númenóreans, had "grown proud, and brooked no power in Middle-earth greater than his own" (66). In this version of the story, imperialism arises within Númenor itself; Its origin is no longer Sauron furthering an imperialist policy, as it was in *The Lost Road* (77). But 'The Drowning of Anadûnê,' written around 1942, returns to the earlier idea that Sauron was behind it all. By his machinations "the king and his men fell under his spell, and hunted the men of Middle-earth and took their goods and enslaved them, and many they slew cruelly on their altars" (*Sauron*, 368). In many ways, then, Tolkien's Númenor shows the same racist attitude to the world as the European imperialists in the 1800s.

Increasingly, then, a desire to hold onto all they have gained is combined with a fear of the unknown, brought on by the erosion of trust in the gift. We can see the resonances in

Tolkien's own Catholic beliefs here. If your belief in God's plan is strong, then fearing and seeking to avoid death is unnecessary as you trust that what comes after death is something good. Unfortunately, it is human nature to fear the unknown, a point acknowledged by Arwen when she must finally face Aragorn's mortality, as well as her own, causing her to reconsider her previous judgement of the people of Númenor. In anguish at what is to come, she laments both her fate and his as, finally, she comes to understand why the Númenóreans may have sought to avoid death, as she tells Aragorn that "not till now have I understood the tale of your people and their fall. As wicked fools I scorned them, but I pity them at last. For if this is indeed, as the Eldar say, the gift of the One to Men, it is bitter to receive" (*RK*, 'Appendix A', 1037-8). Confronted finally with the reality of death and the gift of Ilúvatar, Arwen's faith is tested as sorely as that of any mortal, and she is left to face her own sorrow and despair.

The hubris of Ar-Pharazôn, his overwhelming desire for immortality, and his misunderstanding of the gift of Ilúvatar encourage him to listen to the whisperings of Sauron, who uses the Númenóreans' fear of death as his snare. As a result, he plans to seize the Undying Lands, believing that immortality lay in the land itself rather than in those who live there. Although this leads to the utter destruction of Númenor, he had been sent numerous, explicit warnings that could have changed the fate of Númenor, if he had only heeded them. Caryn L. Cooper & Kevin S. Whetter connect the defiance and the turning away of the Númenóreans from Ilúvatar to the descriptions of the biblical Exodus myth, "establishing Ar-Pharazôn and his King's Men as the Pharaoh and Egyptians of the Akallabêth, while the Faithful are set up as the Hebrews – oppressed and punished by the King's Men for maintaining their faith in the

Valar and in Ilúvatar", pointing to the resonance of certain phrases between the two texts (2020, 3). For example, in the 'Akallabêth', Tolkien describes both Ar-Pharazôn and the people of Númenor as hardening or having hardened their hearts on three occasions, just as, in Exodus, the Pharoah's heart is hardened against the Israelites. Cooper and Whetter note that "both kingdoms also suffer from a pre-emptive divine judgment, with the clear intent of turning the kingdom's actions away from their rebellion against the will of God and the oppression of God's people", prior to a final downfall (3). In Númenor, these include "storms of rain and hail, and violent winds," and lightning, which "increased and slew men upon the hills, and in the fields, and in the streets of the city," and lastly earthquakes and "smoke [which] issued from the peak of the Meneltarma" (*Silmarillion*, 331-2). These portents mirror the plagues sent to Egypt in the Exodus story, particularly the seventh plague where:

> the LORD sent thunder and hail, and fire came down on the earth. And the LORD rained hail on the land of Egypt, [...] hail with fire flashing continually in the midst of it [and] the hail struck down everything that was in the open field throughout all the land of Egypt, both human and animal." (Exod. 9. 23-25)

These warnings, of course, are ignored by both the Pharoah and Ar-Pharazôn, leading to the ultimate destruction by drowning of the respective lands.

So, the Númenóreans bring destruction upon themselves through a combination of hubris, greed, and fear – a fear by which they are trapped as they lose trust in the gift of Ilúvatar. But how does Ilúvatar expect the Númenóreans to simply keep on believing? In Letter 142 to Father Robert Murray, Tolkien admits to having "not put in, or [having] cut out, practically all references to anything like 'religion', to cults or practices" (*Letters*, Letter 142, 257). In a footnote in Letter 153 to Peter Hastings, Tolkien states that "[t]here are thus no temples or 'churches' or fanes in this 'world' among 'good' peoples" and these races "had little or no 'religion' in the sense of worship" (*Letters*, Letter 153, 288-9). If, as Catherine Madsen explains, "the inhabitants of Middle-earth have "no theology, no covenant, and no religious instruction;" they must do "without ritual, revelation, doctrine, indeed without God", what, then, is their relationship with the divine (1988, 43-4)?

The lesson that we are supposed to learn from the Númenóreans' rejection of the gift of death is that mortality is an essential and natural part of the human condition. The Númenóreans' attempts to escape their mortality leads them down a path of arrogance, isolation, and destruction as, led by their pride and conceit, they challenge the authority of the Valar, endeavouring to claim deathlessness for themselves. In an act of defiance against the natural order established by Ilúvatar, the Númenóreans believed that their achievements and power made them equal to the Elves and, as such, entitled to an immortality that they did not fully understand. The end result, of course, is the utter destruction of the Land of Gift, an island raised thousands of years before as a reward for those Edain once recognised as the very best representatives of he human race in Middle-earth, now reduced to slavers, colonisers, and supporters of human sacrifice as an offering to Morgoth in the belief that he would grant them immortality.

Death is indeed a reward; the serial longevity experienced by the Elves (as decreed by Ilúvatar), and by beings such as the Ringwraiths (through unnatural means such as rings of power), comes at a cost. For those whose lives are artificially lengthened, Tolkien tells us that "[t]hey had, as it seemed, unending life, yet life became unendurable to them" (*Silmarillion*, 289). Unending life, even for the Elves, is a burden, and death is a gift "which as Time wears even the Powers shall envy (42). Tolkien's writing suggests that accepting our mortality and the limitation of our human condition is a necessary step towards wisdom, humility, and a deeper appreciation for the gift of life. In this way, the story of the Downfall of Númenor can be read as a cautionary tale about the dangers of trying to escape or deny our mortality, and a reminder to embrace the gift of life while we have it.

Bibliography

Book of Exodus, 9. 23-25. Available at: https://www.bible.com/bible/97/EXO.9.MSG

Cooper, Caryn L. & Whetter, Kevin S., '"Hear, O Númenor!": The Covenantal Relationship of the Dúnedain with Ilúvatar,' *Journal of Tolkien Research*, 11:2, (2020), pp. 1-12.

Garbowski, Christopher, 'Eucatastrophe and the "Gift of Ilúvatar" in Middle-earth' *Mallorn: The Journal of the Tolkien Society*, 35 (1997), pp. 25-32.

Larsen, Kristine, '"Númenor and the "Devouring Wave": Literary, Historical, and Psychological Sources for Tolkien's Self-Described "Atlantis Complex"', *Journal of Tolkien Research*, 11:2, (2020), pp. 1-13.

Madsen, Catherine, 'Light from an Invisible Lamp: Natural Religion in The Lord of the Rings', *Mythlore*, 14: 3, (1988), pp. 43-47.

Purtill, Richard. L., *J. R. R. Tolkien: Myth, Morality, and Religion,* (New York: Harper & Row 1984).

Shippey, Tom, *The Road to Middle-earth*, 2nd ed. (London: HarperCollins, 1992).

Testi, Claudio. 'Tolkien's Legendarium as a Meditatio Mortis,' in *The Broken Scythe: Death and Immortality in the Works of J. R. R. Tolkien*, ed. by Roberto Arduini and Claudio A. Testi, (Zurich: Walking Tree Publishers, 2012).

Tolkien, J. R. R., 'On Fairy-stories' in *The Tolkien Reader*. (New York: Ballantine Books, 1966).
— *The Silmarillion* ed. by Christopher Tolkien. (London: George Allen & Unwin, 1977).
— *The Lost Road and Other Writings: The History of Middle-earth, Volume 5*, ed. by Christopher Tolkien (London: HarperCollins, 1987)
— *Sauron Defeated: The History of Middle-earth, Volume 9*, ed. by Christopher Tolkien. (London: HarperCollins, 1992).
— *Morgoth's Ring: The History of Middle-earth, Volume 10*, ed. by Christopher Tolkien. (London: HarperCollins, 1993).
— *The Peoples of Middle-earth: The History of Middle-earth, Volume 12*, ed. by Christopher Tolkien. (London: HarperCollins, 1996).

—— *Unfinished Tales of Númenor and Middle-earth*, ed. by Christopher Tolkien (London: HarperCollins, 2020).
—— *The Letters of J.R.R. Tolkien, Revised and Expanded Edition*, ed. by Humphrey Carpenter with the assistance of Christopher Tolkien (London: HarperCollins 2023).

ns of the Corporeality of Númenor

Journee Cotton

> Ecological literacy, further, implies a broad understanding of how people and societies relate to each other and to natural systems, and how they might do so sustainably. It presumes both an awareness of the interrelatedness of life and knowledge of how the world works as a physical system. (Orr 2005, 26-7)

As advent of the Anthropocene commenced the significant impact the 'human' has upon the earth's ecology and geology, the narrative people tell about themselves and the world is deeply tied to it. In *Dark Ecology: For a Logic of Future Coexistence* (2018) Timothy Morton observes that generally the Anthropocene is thought of as "nam[ing] two levels we usually think are distinct: geology and humanity" (7). Thus, it is part of this paper's aim to complicate the idea of these two layers, and perhaps, push the boundaries between humanity and the earth to engage more deeply in the interconnectedness of the human, other beings, and the environment. Tolkien's progressive framing of the 'human' in his lore is striking. Instead of taking a heavily anthropocentric perspective Nick Groom notes in 'Nazgûl Taller Than Night: Tolkien and Speculative Realism' (2022) that Tolkien decentred "human agency in his works" and thus "helped to normalize the non-anthropocentric (human-centred) narrative, which had already been developing" (45,

46). By decentring the 'human', the text allows more room and value to be assigned to the other sentient beings dwelling in Middle-earth. This space also allows for a greater engagement with the non-human parts of the world including plants and animals. The environment and its descriptions take notable space in the text and even have roles of agency.

Middle-earth was created as a flat world, but the destructive and unethical actions of the Númenóreans resulted in not only a change in the environment and landscape, but also the world's shape into a globe where: "[a]ll roads are now bent" (*Silmarillion*, 338). Throughout Tolkien's legendarium there is a focus on the physicality of beings and the landscape in connection to their ethical and moral decisions. Númenor offers an example of unethical decisions that have catastrophic consequences on the environment and, ultimately, beings inhabiting the space. My reading of the text uses the interdisciplinary lens of Environmental Bioethics to study corporeality in Tolkien's legendarium. Tolkien's texts are centrally concerned with the idea of death and questions concerning immortality, due to Tolkien's preoccupation with ageing in connection to "serial longevity" and death as an "'escape'" which he considered as the topic *The Lord of the Rings* was "mainly concerned" (*Letters*, Letter 208, 284). This preoccupation seems driven by fear. Anna Milon observes that ultimately the fear of death is replaced by "[t]he fear of decrepitude and barrenness" (2017, 102). This fear of death and degeneration is also a loss of control over the body and the environment. In 'Theorizing in a Space of Ambivalent Openness: Ecocriticism and Ecophobia' (2009) Simon C. Estok notes that "the contempt and fear we feel for the agency of the natural environment needs theorizing" (207). I shall discuss the presence of destruction, death, and the impact on locations to consider the relationship to geography from a holistic perspective on health to demonstrate the connection between the failure of ethics and the detriment of the body of land, and consequently its inhabitants. Thus, the fall of Númenor serves as an excellent example. This paper shall consider the paths that caused the bending of all roads.

I argue that the attempt to erase the vulnerable, weak, and ageing members of their society which resulted in an environmental catastrophe in Númenor and appears to be unfolding again in Gondor may be read from Rob Nixon's lens of "slow violence" (2011, 2). Nixon's 'slow violence' refers to violence of a gradual nature that slowly degrades such as the "long dyings - the staggered and staggeringly discounted casualties, both human and ecological that result from war's toxic aftermaths or climate change - [which] are underrepresented in strategic planning as well as in human memory" (2-3). This plodding destruction is the work of degrees and not typically overtly and instantly cataclysmic. Faramir describes Gondor as "'falling by degrees into dotage'" which situates Gondor as an ageing body that is becoming senile (*TT*, 'The Window on the West', 338). Gondor's misguided approach to death and ageing and the Númenóreans' persistent desire for "'endless life unchanging'" is the same attitude that leads to the loss of the "'old kingdom'" (338). Although the apocalypse of Númenor is not in and of itself a depiction of 'slow violence' the results of it in Gondor are, as Númenóreans attempted to harness power over death by going to the Undying Lands which apocalyptically destroyed the environment they originally inhabited and made them dwell in a degraded space and bodies (Nixon 2011, 2-3). This perspective of and intervention in death situates ageing in their society as an indicator of failure.

Tolkien's legendarium encompasses a variety of textual components he created, such as histories, timelines, invented languages, maps, and even astronomy which serve to provide a greater sense of depth to the space, place, and the reality of Middle-earth. Tolkien's construction of Middle-earth is innately a textual production supported by texts referencing a 'found' history of a distant and scarcely remembered past (*FR*, 'Preface', 19). This history's ecogeography, even to the shape of the earth, is shaped by the catastrophe of Númenor. The failure of ethics of Númenóreans caused the demise of the land of Númenor and the resulting consequences on the environment, animals, humans, and their health. Gerard Hynes notes that as Tolkien wrote mythology, he included "geomythology" in order to develop more fully the historical, fantastic, and literary context of his oeuvre through solidifying it with geological basis as he did in other areas mentioned above (2012, 30). Thus, Númenor serves as an excellent case study to consider as Peter Anthamatten and Helen Hazen explain that health geography "focus[es] on the importance of variations across space, with an emphasis on concepts such as location, direction, and place" (2011, 2). In 'Sustainable Fictions - Geographical, Literary and Cultural Intersections in J.R.R. Tolkien's The Lord of the Rings' (2011) Ina Habermann and Nikolaus Kuhn note that Tolkien created in Middle-earth "an intricate symbolic topography" that "advocat[es] [for] a careful stewardship of the environment" (263, 273). Often in Tolkien's work this advocation for sustainability and environmental facets are expressed by an exploration of extreme negative consequences that arise from the negligence to biotic and environmental factors, as expressed in the tale of Númenor.

The faithful three Houses of Edain "were given wisdom and power and life more enduring than any others of mortal race have possessed" as well as "the Land of Gift" for them to dwell in, also known as Númenor (*Silmarillion*, 311). They were also given a greater length of life than the normal mortal men, yet they did not escape:

> from the doom of death [...] though their years were long, and they knew no sickness, ere the shadow fell upon them. Therefore they grew wise and glorious, and in all things more like to the Firstborn than any other kindreds of Men; and they were tall, taller than the tallest of the sons of Middle-earth; and the light of their eyes was like the bright stars. (311)

The bodies of the inhabitants were imbued in the environment of Númenor with heightened health, as noted in the previous quotation. This effect of the environment on the bodies exhibits features of Anthamatten and Hazen's perspective that "ecological approaches focus on humans as biological entities, recognizing that people are part of interdependent ecological systems" such as "the relationship between humans and their natural and built environments" which means "human-constructed parts of the landscape such as buildings, dams, and roads" (2011, 7, 13). The only apparent limitation put upon the inhabitants was a spatial parameter, that they should not "sail so far westward that the coasts of Númenor could no longer be seen", this parameter was intended to discourage temptation from the immortal aspects of the Blessed Realm (*Silmarillion*, 313).

An example of the connection between the ecological ethical failure in Númenor that has adverse and violent effects on the bodies of the land and beings may be observed when Sauron, dwelling as a hostage in Númenor, rises to influence, and causes "a mighty temple" built in the centre of Númenor, culminating in "the first fire upon the alter Sauron kindled with the hewn wood of Nimloth [a sacred tree] and it crackled and was consumed; […] the land lay under a cloud for seven days" (327-8). The people of Númenor "made sacrifice unto Melkor that he should release them from Death"; they usually chose human sacrifices from amongst the "Faithful" who did not worship Melkor (328). Not only are there ecogeological effects, but this manifestation of violence leads to harm and sacrifice of sentient beings.

Ultimately, Sauron poisons the mind of King Ar-Pharazôn, who in turn breaches the probation to sail west out of sight of Númenor leading to it being:

> utterly destroyed. For it was nigh to the east of the great rift, and its foundations were overturned, and it fell and went down into darkness, and is no more. […] For Illúvatar cast back the Great Seas west of Middle-earth, and the Empty Lands east of it, and new lands and new seas were made; and the world was diminished. (334-5)

According to Tolkien the motivation for the Númenóreans' war "to take the Undying Land by force of a great armada" was "their lust for corporal immortality – which necessitated a catastrophic change in the shape of Earth" (*Letters*, Letter 153, 194). Furthermore, this reinforces the tie between the corporal, degeneration, and even the shape of the earth. The unethical actions on the part of the Númenóreans to try to take immortality by force led to the cataclysmic destruction of Númenor, the gradual degeneration of their bodies as demonstrated in the people of Gondor, and even the change of a flat world to a globe as a boundary to disallow mortals to reach the Undying Lands.

Within the 'Akallabêth', this event is referred as "Atalantë in the Eldarin tongue" (*Silmarillion*, 337); notably, it bares similarities in name and narrative to the Atlantis myth. Tolkien's myth deviates from similarities with the Atlantis myth, as this calamity impacts the rest of the geography of Middle-earth: during this event all coastal regions:

> of the western world suffered great change and ruin in that time; for the seas invaded the lands, and shores floundered, and ancient isles were drowned, and new isles were uplifted; and hills crumbled and rivers were turned into strange courses. (336)

The destruction of Númenor's apocalyptic elements may be best understood through the lens of "[g]eomythology, [which] [...] interprets certain myths and legends in terms of geological events that may have been witnessed by the human cultures who recorded the myths" (Hynes 2012, 28). The destruction, ruin, and "corruption" of Númenor's land, animals, environment, and humans is total; even Sauron's form is "corrupted" during these events (*Silmarillion*, 337). A significant factor of the lasting impact of Númenor's destruction is demonstrated through the Dúnedain's later voyages. The Dúnedain believed in life beyond "those of their bodies' life; and they longed to escape from the shadows of their exile [...] for the sorrow of the thought of death had pursued them over the deeps of the sea [...] But they found it not" (337-8). The Dúnedain and land of Númenor exhibit the close connection between environment and bodies.

There is an embedded connection between the Númenóreans' lust for corporeal immortality and the death and destruction to the bodies of people and Middle-earth. Finally, the nature of the world is changed: the Dúnedain discover from "those that sailed furthest set but a girdle about the Earth and returned weary at last to the place of their beginning; and they said: 'all roads are now bent'" (338). After the fall of Númenor "the world was indeed made round" (338). The ability to physically sail to the undying lands is no longer possible for mortals: Middle-earth's changed form manifestly connects to Howard Brody's conclusion in 'Environmental and Global Issues' (2009) that the environment and inhabitant's "well-being" are intrinsically tied: "[i]f the environment is degraded, our lives, our futures, and our children's existence are all threatened" (177). This paper offers a reading of Tolkien's legendarium through an interdisciplinary framework of Health Geography and Environmental Bioethics to consider the lust after corporeal immortality in an attempt to evade death that is legible in the body of place and beings of the people of Númenor. Although our roads exist on a globe, perhaps the destruction wrecked on the planet are 'bending' pathways due to unethical environmental action, such as environmentally harmful modes of travel and acts of 'slow violence' that have real bioethical consequences on bodies and have also altered the pathways we take now. There may come a day that our pathways are altered owing to our treatment of the environment due to the rise of ocean waters, the scarcity of resources, or the degradation of environments affecting human health and welfare. May we heed the tale of the drowning of Númenor.

Bibliography

Anthamatten, Peter, and Helen Hazen, *An Introduction to the Geography of Health*, (London: Routledge, 2011).

Brody, Howard, 'Environmental and Global Issues', in *The Future of Bioethics*, (Oxford: Oxford University Press, 2009), pp. 177-192, ProQuest Ebook Central, https://ebookcentral.proquest.com/lib/bristol/detail.action?docID=2012750 [Accessed 30 September 2021]

Estok, Simon C., 'Theorizing in a Space of Ambivalent Openness: Ecocriticism and Ecophobia', *Interdisciplinary Studies in Literature and Environment*, 16.2, (2009), pp. 203–25. JSTOR, http://www.jstor.org/stable/44733418 [Accessed 10 April 2023]

Gaston, Kevin J., et al, 'Ecogeographical Rules: Elements of a Synthesis', *Journal of Biogeography*, 35.3, (2008), pp. 483–500. JSTOR, http://www.jstor.org/stable/30054709 [Accessed 19 April 2023]

Groom, Nick, 'Nazgûl Taller Than Night: Tolkien and Speculative Realism' in *Twenty-first Century Receptions of Tolkien: Proceedings of the Tolkien Society Winter Seminar 2021*, ed. by Will Sherwood, (Edinburgh: Luna Press, 2022), pp. 38-57.

Habermann, Ina, and Nikolaus Kuhn, 'Sustainable Fictions - Geographical, Literary and Cultural Intersections in J.R.R. Tolkien's The Lord of the Rings', *Cartographic Journal*, 48.4, (2011), pp. 263–273. *EBSCOhost*, https://www-tandfonline-com.uoelibrary.idm.oclc.org/doi/full/10.1179/1743277411Y.0000000024 [Accessed 07 October 2021]

Hynes, Gerard, '"Beneath the Earth's dark keel": Tolkien and Geology', *Tolkien Studies*, pp. 21-36, (2012), https://doi.org/10.1353/tks.2012.0005 [Accessed 11 October 2021]

Milon, Anna, 'Mortal immortals: the fallibility of elven immortality in Tolkien's writing', in *Death and Immortality in Middle-earth: proceedings of the Tolkien Society Seminar 2016*, ed. by Daniel Helen, (Edinburgh: Luna Press Publishing, 2017), pp. 99-108.

Morton, Timothy, *Dark Ecology: For a Logic of Future Coexistence*, (New York: Columbia University Press, 2018).

Nixon, Rob, *Slow Violence and the Environmentalism of the Poor*, (Cambridge: Harvard University Press, 2011). JSTOR, http://www.jstor.org/stable/j.ctt2jbsgw [Accessed 11 July 2022]

Orr, David, 'Ecological Literacy', *The Earthscan Reader in Sustainable Agriculture*, ed. by Jules Pretty, (London: Earthscan, 2005), pp. 21–29.

Tolkien, J.R.R., *The Fellowship of the Ring*, (New York: The Ballantine Publishing Group, 1994).
— *The Silmarillion*, ed. by Christopher Tolkien, 2nd edn (New York: Del Rey, 2001).
— *The Two Towers*, (New York: The Ballantine Publishing Group, 1994).
— *The Letters of J.R.R. Tolkien*, ed. by Humphrey Carpenter with the assistance of Christopher Tolkien, (London: Houghton Mifflin Harcourt, 2014).

Ecology of Imperialism: Environmental History for Númenor

Muhammed Alpaslan Tandırcı

In *General Morphology* (1886), Ernst Haeckel categorises ecology as a sub-discipline of biology. Since, it has grown to become a separate branch of science that interacts with the social sciences, of which environmental history is just one. According to Andrew Isenberg, Donald Worster defined environmental history in 1988 as "the interactions people have had with nature in past times" (2014, 4). What is meant by the concept of state here is not the distinction between the modern state, kingdom, or primitive state structures, but an administrative organisation of a political nature. For example, J.R.R. Tolkien's legendarium does not include a state structure with legislative, executive, and judicial powers and a constitution, rather there is a king or queen whose authority over their kingdom mimics that of Middle Age rulers. This is what is meant by the state and modernity.

States are among the important actors of environmental history research because they are established in geography and the environment; consequently they are both affected by and affect the environment. From this point of view, analysing the environmental effects of the policies implemented by states is one of the important points for environmental history. In addition, forests, seas, and rivers play an important role in the analysis of environmental history. For example, Joachim

Radkau emphasises the importance of forests with examples such as Egyptian Pharaohs and German Princes (2020, 232-3, 516). Alan Mikhail, on the other hand, sees states as ecosystems, explaining the importance of lumbering and forests in Ottoman history (2019, 234, 11-2). Environmental history research also has a catastrophic dimension because a state's relationship with the environment does not always end happily. In some cases, states have collapsed due to environmental factors such as in the case of Easter Island (Ponting 2012, 2-3).

Tolkien's legendarium has strong ecological connections and historical structures. When we review the history of Middle-earth, we understand that there are different time periods such as the time of the Lamps, Years of the Trees, and the time of the Sun and Moon. Tolkien even explains the differences in units of time between these periods. When this explanation is taken as a reference, it is understood that thousands of years of Middle-earth history were written (*Nature*, 22). There are many studies about this as nature and the environment are central to Tolkien's work. It is possible to see this reflected in his letters, such as his letter from 30 June 1972: "in all my works I take the part of trees as against all their enemies" (*Letters*, Letter 339, 419). Tolkien's works were even one of the inspirations for the ecological movement of the 1960s (Curry 2007a, 165). For Patrick Curry, nature is more like a character than decor (2007b, 453). However, history and historicity are also very important to Tolkien and Middle-earth marries ecology with history in an original approach. This paves the way for an environmental historical analysis of Middle-earth. For the sake of this paper, it is necessary to refer to the legendarium's events as real within the fictional sphere of the secondary world. The paper will focus on the Kingdom of Númenor as an example for this framework of study.

In general, the concept of imperialism, which comes from the Latin root *imperium*, is the attempt of a state or nation to influence other states or nations (Onions 1994, 464). Imperialism, then, can be used as a state policy. However, the place of influence is not a specific country or nation, but a region: Middle-earth. Therefore the ecology of imperialism refers to the interactions between a state's strategy or policy with the environment. When Númenor's imperial policies are examined chronologically from an ecological perspective, an environmental history will be made. This study starts with the assumption that Middle-earth has a strong historical structure. In a way, this is also ecocritical because Númenor is a literary country. This study does not seek to analyse the flora-fauna and biogeography of Númenor. To analyse the environmental history of Númenor is to examine not an island but the state, its policies over time, and the consequences of these policies on the environment.

1 - The Start of Imperial Ambition in Aldarion and Erendis

Between the early days of the Second Age and the founding of Númenor, to the time of 'Aldarion and Erendis: The Mariner's Wife', the Númenóreans established a political system that suited the island nation. However, by the time of Aldarion, Númenor had started to expand its scope beyond its borders to Middle-earth.

During these years, Númenor did not practise a despotic policy. They were curious, adventurous, and exploratory, needing timber to build more ships as the island's resources were limited. It was King Meneldur, when Aldarion was still a prince, who passed a law against cutting down trees on the island of Númenor because of the shortage (*UT*, 295). This is important in terms of the relationship between law and the environment as Aldarion and his men later harmed Middle-earth through lumbering; however, their intentions were not evil. In addition, cities established during Aldarion's explorations are not castles.

One of the important themes in this narrative is logging and worldview. The point to be emphasized here is that Aldarion and Erendis have different worldviews, values, and perspectives. Through this difference, Tolkien may have wanted to give a preliminary message that the Kingdom of Númenor's maritime explorations would have negative consequences (like the 'Akallabêth'). However, the difference of opinion of these two characters did not come out of nowhere. With a flow of events, we see two people who love each other drifting apart, representing differing views. Erendis becomes a factor here as she is against the felling of trees. For example, she has a conservative side because she is afraid to leave her homeland and of innovation. Aldarion is open to innovations and wants to travel to new places. It is possible to see some examples of this here:

> but she feared now in her heart that in the war between herself and the Sea for the keeping of Aldarion she would not conquer. Never would Erendis take less, that she might not lose all; and fearing the Sea, and begrudging to all ships the felling of trees which she loved, she determined that she must utterly defeat the Sea and the ships, or else be herself defeated utterly. (182)

It is clear that Erendis is at a crossroads in her thoughts. She both wants Aldarion and is saddened by the cutting down of the trees in the land she loves. The continuation of this state of sadness will turn into her hostility towards the sea, exploration and ideologies related to Aldarion's worldview. However, despite her fears she consented to go to sea with Aldarion (182). This did not conclude well as

> there Valandil, Lord of Andunie and close kin of Aldarion, held a great feast; and at that feast he drank to Erendis, naming her Uineniel, Daughter of Uinen, the new Lady of the Sea. But Erendis, who sat beside the wife of Valandil, said aloud: 'Call me by no such name! I am no daughter of Uinen: rather is she my foe.' (182)

Here Erendis's attitude towards the sea seems to have strengthened due to Aldarion's exploits. Erendis initially did not think negatively about the seas; however, Aldarion's fondness for it and neglect of Erendis and his duties on Númenor changed Erendis's view.

Erendis strove to bring Aldarion to love the land: "will you not journey with me ashore, to the places that I love? You know too little of this land, for one who shall be its King" (182). Aldarion agrees and the result is the practice of planting new trees to account for those felled. This is similar to the 'Polluter Pays Principle' in ecological literature: in order to reduce the damage to nature, there should be a price to pay (Turgut 1995, 619). In the case of Númenor, planting new trees is in keeping with ecological theory. Erendis represents land, earth, and conservation, all of which are fixed, static, and unmoving. Aldarion on the other hand represents water, sea, and societal progress, symbolizing exploration and movement.

These worldviews resonate with Carl Schmitt's arguments in *Land and Sea: A World-Historical Meditation*. Schimitt and Númenor converge Aldarian's transformation of Númenor into a maritime empire that utilises sea power (2015, 11). Before

Aldarion, Númenor was a state that looked inward. Aldarion looked outward and expanded the island's empire to Umbar and beyond. However, if Aldarion had adhered to Erendis's conservative views, Númenor might have remained an introverted island nation. As a result of Aldarion's interventions at home, colonialism and imperialism started to look more appealing.

2 - The Glamour of Exploration: Colonisation

Númenor established colonies on the southern shores of Middle-earth for economic interests. Thanks to Lond Dear (Vinyalondë) and Tharbad, the Númenóreans were able to target forests for timber for shipbuilding. Colonisation comes from the Latin root *colónus*, which means to cultivate the land (Onions 1994, 192). The Númenóreans did not consider Middle-earth their homeland so they targeted Eriador's natural resources. The people here are diverse communities other than the Edain (Straubhaar 2007, 415). Númenor's policies are expansionist and colonial, but not capitalist. It is important to recognise this boundary as Eriador is the region where Númenor's influence is most evident. Eriador is geographically suitable for this as there are no mountain ranges between it and the sea and the river mouths in the south make it easy to access. This is why the Númenóreans founded Vinyalondë and then consolidated it with Tharbard. The Númenóreans could not achieve a similar effect east of the Misty Mountains because the White Mountains were a natural barrier.

It took 1680 years for Númenor's colonialism to become despotic. This transformation is shown between the establishing of Vinyalondë (which represents exploration), and Umbar (which represents imperial desires and despotism). Númenor's despotism can be seen through three actions: ships carrying jewellery and minerals from Middle-earth back to Númenor, slavery, and human sacrifice. They are the result of the Númenóreans growing greed, as is the damage wreaked on Middle-earth.

3 - The Bitter End of Glamour: Deforestation

Middle-earth remained relatively untouched in the First Age as the lands to the east of Ered Luin were not the setting for the War of Wrath. However, there are references in *The Silmarillion* and *The Lord of the Rings* to the existence of an ancient and extensive forest system in Middle-earth which is located between the Blue Mountains and the Misty Mountains. In the latter, the Old Forest is said to be: "ancient, a survivor of vast forgotten woods; and in it there lived yet, ageing no quicker than the hills, the fathers of the fathers of trees, remembering times when they were lords" (*FR*, 'In the House of Tom Bombadil', 130). Similarly, Treebeard tells Merry and Pippin about the vast forests of Middle-earth: "'It is rather a strange and sad story,' he went on after a pause. 'When the world was young, and the woods were wide and wild, the Ents and the Entwives – and there were Entmaidens then'" (*TT*, 'Treebeard', 475).

However, the maps of the Third Age indicate that these ancient systems shrank into the Old Forest, Fangorn, Lothlórien, and Mirkwood (Fonstad 1991, 53). Treebeard's reminiscences evince that it is the Númenóreans and their wars with Sauron that are partially to blame for Middle-earth's ecological devastation: "I remember it was long ago – in the time of the war between Sauron and the Men of the Sea – desire came over me to see Fimbrethil again" (*TT*, 'Treebeard', 476). Although on opposing sides, the resulting catastrophe is an ecological evil enacted by the Númenóreans as well as Sauron. Additionally, Sauron's assault on Eriador in the Second Age is so devastating because the Númenóreans cut down Eriador's forest, leaving great clearings for Mordor's armies to advance without hindrance. This further stretched into the Third Age, as the fall of Arnor was also partially because of the wasteland the Númenóreans created. Arnor was founded on fragile and open geography. It could not, therefore, become a mighty and wealthy state because of its weak roots.

These crises could have been avoided if the Númenóreans had cooperated more with the Elves. The forests would have potentially not been cut down and natural borders would not have been damaged. In addition, the people of Middle-earth and Númenor could have united and formed a powerful political force against Sauron. Alternatively, Elves and Men could have regenerated the forests but there is no evidence of any attempt. This can be explained through the level of civilisation and population. Due to geographical fragility, low populations, and the war of the Last Alliance, Eregion suffered and collapsed from political instability and inaction. In fact, it would not be erroneous to say that Arnor was a terrestrial or steppe state – not in a nomadic sense. Reforestation, like deforestation, is political and cannot be done individually as it has to be organised through a state. This is also mentioned in *The Fall of Númenor*:

> Valandil took up his abode in Annúminas, but his folk were diminished, and of the Númenóreans and of the Men of Eriador there remained now too few to people the land or to maintain all the places that Elendil had built; in Dagorlad, and in Mordor, and upon the Gladden Fields many had fallen. (*FoN*, 289)

In conclusion, the forests of Middle-earth were badly damaged not only by Sauron but by the Númenóreans. Besides their policy of deforestation, the wars during the Second Age further damaged Middle-earth's environment, evincing that human action lends itself to evil consequences. During Númenor's imperialism, Middle-earth lost its forests (especially in Eriador), biodiversity was damaged, and Eriador was vulnerable to Sauron's forces. Númenor's alienation from both its own nature and the nature of Middle-earth not only brought about its own downfall, but that of Middle-earth itself for ages to come.

Bibliography

Curry, Patrick, 'Environmentalism and Eco-Criticism' in *J. R. R. Tolkien Encyclopedia: Scholarship And Critical Assessment*, ed. by Michael D. C. Drout (New York: Routledge, 2007a), p. 165.
— 'Nature' in *J. R. R. Tolkien Encyclopedia: Scholarship And Critical Assessment*, ed. by Michael D. C. Drout (New York: Routledge, 2007b), p. 453.

Fonstad, Karen Wynn, *The Atlas of Middle-earth*, (Boston: Houghton Mifflin Company, 1991).

Isenberg, Andrew C., 'Introduction: A New Environmental History' in *The Oxford Handbook of Environmental History*, ed. by Andrew C. Isenberg (Oxford: Oxford University Press, 2014), pp. 1-22.

Mikhail, Alan, *Osman'ın Ağacı Altında: Osmanlı İmparatorluğu, Mısır ve Çevre Tarihi*, (İstanbul: İş Bankası Kültür Yayınları, 2019).

Onions, C. T., *The Oxford Dictionary of English Etymology*, ed. by C. T. Onions with the assistance of G. W. S. Friedrichsen and R. W. Burchfield (New York: Oxford University Press Inc., 1994).

Ponting, Clive, *Dünyanın Yeşil Tarihi*, (İstanbul: Sabancı Üniversitesi Yayınları, 2008).

Radkau, Joachim, *Doğa ve İktidar: Global Bir Çevre Tarihi*, (İstanbul: İş Bankası Kültür Yayınları, 2017).

Schmitt, Carl, *Land and Sea: A World-Historical Meditation*, (New York: Telos Press Publishing, 2015).

Straubhaar, S.B., 'Men, Middle-earth' in *J. R. R. Tolkien Encyclopedia: Scholarship And Critical Assessment*, ed. by Michael D. C. Drout (New York: Routledge, 2007), p. 415.

Tolkien, J. R. R., *Unfinished Tales of Númenor and Middle-earth*, (Boston: Houghton Mifflin Company Boston, 1980).
— *The Lord of the Rings*, (London: HarperCollins, 1994). 50th anniversary edition.
— *The Letters of J.R.R. Tolkien*, ed. Humphrey Carpenter with the assistance

of Christopher Tolkien (London: HarperCollins, 2006).
— *The Nature of Middle-earth*, ed. by Carl Hostetter (London: HarperCollins, 2021). Kindle edition.
— *The Fall of Númenor*, ed. by Brian Sibley (London: HarperCollins, 2023). Kindle edition.

Turgut, Nükhet, 'Kirleten Öder İlkesi ve Çevre Hukuku', *Ankara Üniversitesi Hukuk Fakültesi Dergisi*, 44.1. (1995), 607-654.

The 'Akallabêth' and the Anthropocene: Myth, Ecology, and the Changing of the World

Erik Jampa Andersson

This paper explores how critical analysis of Tolkien's tale of Númenor can help shed light on the social, ecological, and political dynamics of the Anthropocene. While the tragedy of the *Atalantë* usually centres around the dramatic cataclysm of SA 3319, the roots of this process lie deep in Númenor's history, arising through waves of expanding exploitation, domination, and disenchantment. Much like primary-world colonial powers, the Númenóreans enriched themselves through ecocide, genocide, slave labour, and colonisation to make important technological and military advances throughout the Second Age. But in their pursuit of "Peak Humanity" they became increasingly vulnerable to Sauron's promises of ultimate sovereignty and limitless 'progress' – and much like the European colonial pursuit of supreme dominance, their hubris ultimately triggered catastrophic planetary consequences (Grove 2015).

In 1965 Tolkien wrote that, while "the days of the bliss of Númenor [...] lasted for well nigh two thousand years [...] the first hints of the latter shadows appeared before that [...] Victory was the herald of their Downfall" (*Nature*, 340). This insight provides critical nuance to the standard Númenórean narrative. While the cataclysm is elsewhere described as having occurred "[i]n an hour unlooked for by Men" (340), the *Atalantë* was not an unprecedented or unforeseen event – it had, much like the Anthropocene, been many years in the making. While the applicability of the Númenórean mythos to the Anthropocene has hitherto been almost entirely overlooked in Tolkien scholarship, I argue that such investigations can provide valuable clarity to the narrativization of our drowning world.

I do not intend to reduce Númenor's fall to an allegory of the Anthropocene – besides being fundamentally contrary to Tolkien's creative disposition, the notion of the 'Anthropocene' is anachronistic. Nevertheless, his astute and perennial critique of industrialisation, exploitation, and instrumentalism places his work well within the purview of modern ecocriticism. He did not need the abundant data we now possess to formulate a critical opinion of colonisation, ecocide, or industrial 'progress.' Furthermore, Tolkien notably spent a great deal of time pondering the dynamics of an 'Age of Men,' including its dependence upon a fall from enchantment. As the history of Númenor demonstrates, it was precisely such a 'fall' that led to the tragedy of the *Atalantë*.

1 - On History and Historiography

History is a powerful form of storytelling, and its composition is never neutral. The intentions, ideologies, and values of historians often have a significant impact on the plots, styles, tropes, and modes of storytelling employed in historiography, comprising what Hayden White terms the metahistorical dimensions of a historical work (1973, ix-x). Approaching Tolkien's writings through a historical lens demands that we carefully consider these dynamics in both the 'external' and 'internal' compositional layers of his work. Tolkien's predisposition towards 'historical' modes of storytelling is well-attested. As he writes, "I cordially dislike allegory in all its manifestations […] I much prefer history, true or feigned, with its varied applicability to the thought and experience of readers" (*FR*, 'Foreward to the Second Edition', 11). While these words are normally cited to illustrate his contempt for allegory, Tolkien's astute grasp on historiography is often underappreciated. He goes on to say, "an author cannot of course remain wholly unaffected by his experience, but the ways in which a story-germ uses the soil of experience are extremely complex" (11). This insight is every bit as applicable to the historian's craft as it is to the writing of fiction, and Tolkien's understanding of this dynamic is itself part of what makes his narratives so rich.

It is still important to remember that he constructed his legendarium as a collection of primary and secondary 'historical' documents: some, like *The Hobbit* and *The Lord of the Rings*, are identifiable as first- and second-hand accounts composed by figures like Frodo and Bilbo Baggins; while others are positioned as historical, philosophical, or philological tracts from Elvish and Human lore-masters of the distant past. Because of his careful attentiveness to this dynamic, the 'sources' that Tolkien presents are deliberately primed for historical interrogation. Internal bias, guesswork, propaganda, and falsification are all observable in the primary texts themselves. The internal authors of these works were very much 'unreliable narrators' – some were even 'historians' themselves, imperfectly attempting to piece together historical narratives from their own scanty 'evidence.'

Tolkien's 'external' composition of the Númenórean mythos spanned four decades, with pivotal works on the Downfall written in three main phases. The first layer emerged around 1936, when Númenor first appeared in 'The Lost Road', leading ultimately to the composition of 'The Fall of Númenor'. The second layer, 'The Drowning of Anadûnê' emerged circa 1945-1946 along with the composition of 'The Notion Club Papers' and 'Lowdham's Report on the Adunaic language'. The third layer emerged around the mid-1950s with the 'Akallabêth' proper, which later became established as the 'canonical' version of the tale included in *The Silmarillion*. As Christopher Tolkien demonstrates in *Sauron Defeated*, these core works were ultimately taken to represent three distinct layers of Númenórean historiography: an "Elvish tradition" in 'The Fall of Númenor', a "Mannish tradition" in 'Drowning of Anadûnê', and a "mixed Dúnedanic tradition" in 'Akallabêth' (406). 'Internally' the former two were composed first, likely around the end of the Second Age, while the 'Akallabêth' was written not long thereafter. At one point, Tolkien records Elendil as the internal author of the latter text, though this is never elsewhere attested (*UT*, 242, 246).

The "Elvish" account in 'The Fall of Númenor' mainly attributes the Downfall to Sauron, who compelled the otherwise virtuous Númenóreans to defy the ban of the Valar. Their "imperial ambition" is principally directed towards Valinor in this early layer (Hynes 2013, 125). This approach predominated Tolkien's perception of Númenórean history until 'The Drowning of Anadûnê'. This alternative "Mannish" tradition shed more nuanced light on Númenor's corruption, demonstrating that imperialistic ambitions and a lust for global dominance were present from at least the early days of Ar-Pharazôn's reign, and that Sauron needed only to exploit these ambitions to facilitate Númenor's ruin (126).

Both of these texts were clearly consulted for the composition of the 'Akallabêth', or the "mixed Dúnedanic" tradition, and the

Appendices– both of which Tolkien penned around the early-to-mid 1950s. Taken together, these narratives shift the roots of Númenórean corruption even further into the past – this time over 1500 years, to the reigns of the twelfth king, Tar-Ciryatan, and the thirteenth king, Tar-Atanamir (*Silmarillion*, 265). But in the Appendices (internally composed at the beginning of the Fourth Age), it's noted that Númenor began building "permanent havens" in Middle-earth as early as 1200, and by the time of the eleventh king Tar-Minastir, they had already begun "to establish dominions on the coasts" (*RK*, 'Appendix B', 1120). In contrast to the narratives provided in the Mannish and Elvish traditions, these later chronicles demonstrate that Númenor's descent into imperialism began long before Ar-Pharazôn ascended the throne, Before the Númenóreans decided to try and seize deathlessness from the gods, they spent millennia attempting to contrive it through conquest and world domination.

While they do not deal with the cataclysm itself, works like 'A Description of the Island of Númenor', 'Aldarion and Erendis: The Mariner's Wife', and 'Tal-Elmar' (externally composed between 1950-1968) provide additional context regarding the root causes of Númenor's eventual fall. The 'Description' and related texts offer a detailed overview of Númenor's environmental history based on records and maps found in Gondor's archives. In these works, ancient relations between Númenor's Human and non-Human are highlighted, demonstrating the great care with which they once related to the animals, plants, and other beings in their midst. This heightens the tragedy of 'The Mariner's Wife', written by Tolkien around the same time, which tells of Aldarion, the sixth King of Númenor, and the widespread deforestation and colonisation efforts that he initiated. Importantly, Tolkien identified this text as one of the few surviving histories composed in Númenor itself, "preserved in the Downfall [...] because it tells how Númenor became involved in the politics of Middle-earth" (*Letters*, Letter 276, 360) – making it a valuable source of primary historical evidence. Hynes describes it as "the fall of Númenor in microcosm," narrating the critical "turning point" in Númenórean values (2013, 132).

By the end of his life, Tolkien regarded the *Atalantë* as a long and complicated process, beginning no later than the 9th century and culminating in the cataclysm of the 34th century. This diverges quite substantially from his earlier works, as well as the so-called 'standard narrative' regarded as 'canon.' But rather than positioning these variant works as 'draft' or 'canonical' versions of a single tale, it is far more accurate – and certainly more interesting – to view each as discrete historical narratives internally penned by an array of imperfect authors and scholars over the millennia. In this light, just as a historian's perspective on the past may evolve with the discovery of new sources, Tolkien's narrativization of Númenor's fall evolved with additional data.

2 - *Atalantë* and the Changing of the Earth

While simplistic accounts of the *Atalantë* tend to place the greatest blame on Sauron, critical historical analysis demonstrates that, by the time he was brought to Númenor as Ar-Pharazôn's hostage, Númenor's fall had already been in motion for millennia. As Hynes notes, over time the story "would become more than the sudden breaking of a prohibition, turning instead into a study in the causes and consequences of human corruption" (2013, 124).

In their infancy, the peoples of Númenor demonstrated a great deal of wisdom and promise – in addition to their friendship with the Elves and allegiance to the Valar, they maintained respectful social relations with many kinds of non-Human beings. Tolkien writes that "the relations of Men and animals remained more friendly in Númenor than anywhere else in the world" (*Nature*, 334). Even bears made meaningful contributions to Númenórean culture, performing their Great Bear-dance (*ruxoälë*) every autumn "for the entertainment of their human friends" (*FoN*, 20), and sociable bonds were also maintained with foxes, rabbits, urchins, eagles, and numerous other creatures. The Númenóreans primarily subsisted on a pescatarian and plant-based diet (18-22), with any necessary hunts (usually targeting overpopulous predators) executed "within limits" in the manner of ritualised warfare, providing "due warning" to the animals before their pursuit (18).

But things changed over time, and Númenórean relations with other Human and non-Human beings gradually deteriorated. As noted by scholars like Hynes and Katrine L. A. Hjulstad, *deforestation* was an important early step in this devolution, as seen in 'The Mariner's Wife'. This text recounts how Aldarion founded the Guild of Venturers, a league of seafarers dedicated to the exploration of Middle-earth. His father, the fifth king Tar-Meneldur, was ever-wary of his son's ambitions, fearing that he was sowing "the seeds of restlessness and the desire of other lands to hold" (*UT*, 193). He was also evidently concerned about the ecological impact of Aldarion's naval fleet, especially on Númenor's forests, leading him to ultimately ban all logging on the island (194-7). Undeterred, Aldarion turned his sights to the forests of Middle-earth as a 'resource' for his ships, and established the haven at Vinyalondë (194).

In the 9th century, the mass deforestation of Eriador began. While Aldarion was once careful about "planting always where there was felling" (208), this ethic ultimately waned, and under his direction the Númenóreans are reported to have "become ruthless in their fellings, giving no thought to husbandry or replanting" (281-2), with many of his peers and subjects (including his wife) worrying that "he had little love for trees in themselves, caring for them rather as timber that would serve his designs" (208). Of course, the building of ships did not simply lead to the destruction of trees, but also the conquest and subjugation of lands and peoples through the expansion of the empire. This notably included the dispossession and enslavement of the so-called "lesser Men" of Middle-earth (*RK*, 'Appendix A', 1073), a pejorative taxonomy that was itself devised by the Númenóreans based largely on perceptions of physical and social difference (*Peoples*, 312-4). Many of these peoples were scattered forest-dwelling communities with no centralised leadership (*UT*, 281), including the Gwaithuirim and the people of Agar, to whom we'll return later.

Whatever respectful social bonds the Númenóreans had once maintained with other Human and non-Human beings, these relationships deteriorated into dynamics of instrumentalist exploitation in Aldarion's time, and by the 19th century, Númenor had become a formidable colonial superpower with remarkable wealth and geopolitical influence along the western coasts of Middle-earth (*RK*, 'Appendix B', 1120). By the time Ar-Pharazôn usurped the throne in the 33rd century, the "shadow" had already been present in Númenor for well over a thousand years (*RK*, 'Appendix B', 1120), with the primitive accumulation of natural resources and exploitation of slave labour allowing them to grow into one of the most powerful forces the world had ever known (*Silmarillion*, 290). The mere fact that they could effectively challenge Sauron for global domination speaks volumes to the sheer magnitude of their might. Of course, the temporary 'defeat' of Sauron ultimately led to grave consequences, allowing him to stoke Ar-Pharazôn's ruthless ambition to 'compass' Númenor's ruin (290).

The Númenórean cataclysm is said to have forever altered the once-flat Earth into a sphere as Valinor was removed beyond the reach of Men and all paths that once ran to the uttermost West now "led nowhere but back again" (*Sauron*, 410). But as attested in his essay 'Myths Transformed' (late 1950s), Tolkien seems to have regarded this 'flat Earth' trope as a "Mannish myth" – an internally fictitious motif based on Human misapprehensions of reality (*Morgoth*, 370). Seeds of this dynamic were notably present even in the earliest layers of the Númenórean mythos, with 'The Drowning of Anadûne' positioning the idea of a flat Earth as a lie devised by Sauron: "and he bade men think that the world was not a circle closed, but there lay many seas and lands for their winning, wherein was wealth uncounted" (*Sauron*, 367). After the cataclysm, Tolkien notes that many came to believe (falsely) that the Earth had been made round by the gods only "in the time of the great Downfall," and that it "was not thus before" (395).

However, the most dramatic and devastating transformations of the Earth had been occurring throughout the Second Age– largely at the hands of the Númenóreans themselves. The deforestation of the coastlands of Middle-earth was itself an active Earth-changing process with widespread consequences for countless beings, and the elimination and expulsion of indigenous peoples from these lands was nothing short of apocalyptic for those whose lifeways were being severed. It is precisely due to attempts "to seize world-power and immortality by force" that the Númenórean empire fell, leading to the sundering of mortal lands – at least in *principle* – from the blissful realm of the gods (*Letters*, Letter 154, 198).

Disenchantment and geological change were not mere sideeffects of the pursuit of domination, but rather the very terms of its attainment: Númenórean ambition "necessitated," in Tolkien's words, "a catastrophic change in the shape of Earth" (*Letters*, Letter 153, 194).

The Númenóreans always intended to change the world through the expansion of their own power – but rather conveniently, many unsavoury details of this project were forgotten (or omitted) by later historians. By the end of the Third Age, Tolkien notes that "all but a few regarded study of what was left of [Númenor's] history as vain, breeding only useless regret [...] The story of Ar-Pharazôn and his impious armada was all that remained generally known" (*UT*, 181). Given their ongoing war against Sauron, it is perhaps unsurprising that they might seek to construct a narrative of the past that amplifies the culpability of their yet-enduring enemy. In this light, the possibility that Elendil had anything at all to do with the composition of the 'Akallabêth' is itself quite notable (242). In the narrativization of history, the propagandic reimagining of the past to support contemporary political aims has often been the norm.

3 - The Tale of the Anthropocene

The term Anthropocene – the 'Epoch of Humans' – was coined by biologist Eugene Stoermer and atmospheric scientist Paul Crutzen to define a new geological epoch "dominated by human activity," marked by widespread "anthropogenic changes to the earth's lithosphere, biosphere, atmosphere, and hydrosphere" (Schneiderman 2017, 170). While geologists agree that we are indeed already in this new geological epoch attempts to establish its inception, causes, and a satisfactory name have been notoriously contentious. While epochs are formally geological conventions, the Anthropocene is far more than a scientific theory: it is a story demanding world-altering transformations in our understanding of ecology, history, nature, culture, and what it means to be Human.

The quest for the inaugural 'golden spike' marking the Anthropocene's emergence has led researchers to three pivotal periods: the Great Acceleration of the mid-20th century, the Industrial Revolution of the 18th century, and the dawn of the European colonial era in the 'long' 16th century (Yusoff 2018, 21-3). However, the historical intricacy and interrelatedness of these 'spikes' undermine a strictly empirical and geological approach to the epoch. Merely locating a transition in the fossil record does little to explain the complex cultural, socio-political, and historical contexts that provoked it. However, to truly understand the Anthropocene's origins and respond to its challenges, social and environmental histories are every bit as crucial as geological data.

Taking the Colonial Era as a significant early 'stage' of the Anthropocene's progression, it is notable that, much like Númenor, mass deforestation was an important early step in this process. Once-thriving Mediterranean woodlands were likewise razed to the ground for the building of imperial fleets, which were used for exploration/conquest and the global transportation of livestock, stolen goods, and enslaved peoples (Williams 2006, 127-8). But as Michael Williams notes, "the attitudes toward the forest that drove the desire to clear in Europe also drove clearing in the new settlements, especially in North America" (128), leading to the terraforming of much of the 'discovered' world into a storehouse of European resources, the primitive accumulation of which was closely linked to indigenous dispossession, genocide, and the exploitation of slave labour. These developments were crucial preconditions for the European Industrial Revolution and the establishment of our modern capitalist economy, which in turn facilitated the Great Acceleration of the 20th century.

Beyond its name and chronology, the story of the Anthropocene makes some bold assertions about the world in which we live, including the reduction of 'Humanity' to an undifferentiated whole. The designation of the 'Anthropo-cene' is itself built upon this assumption, with some claiming that the epoch demands a shift towards a kind of "negative universal history", transcending social and political nuances to highlight our collective culpability as a fundamentally destructive species (Chakrabarty 2009, 220-2). This story pays little heed to the fact that not all Humans have been the aggressors: the 50+ million indigenous Americans killed in the 16th century were not a part of some undifferentiated ecocidal 'Anthropos,' nor were the countless others who were obliterated or enslaved over the past 500 years. This is a depoliticising narrative, designed to generalise blame and obscure the specific historical, social, and cultural dynamics that laid the foundations of our epoch (Bonneuil and Fressoz 2015, 72-9).

Much like the Dúnedanic story of the 'Earth made round,' the Anthropocene narrative also posits that the 'changing of the Earth' was a largely unintentional and modern process with no precedent or warning. We are told that pre-modern Humans had minimal impact on the so-called 'natural' world. This 'shock' narrative suggests that it was only in the past 70 years that the changes became significant enough for us to comprehend, and respond to, the consequences of our actions, but even Tolkien's work itself demonstrates that this is simply not true. Critics have been speaking out against the perils of industrialisation, colonisation, and ecocide for centuries –

we simply failed to listen. Now, when things have become increasingly dire, many claim that we should embrace the Anthropocene as an opportunity for even more control and dominance. Just as narratives of the *Atalantë* were whitewashed to bolster opposition against Sauron's empire, the story of the Anthropocene is used to justify the expansion of Human control for a more utopian (but fundamentally unchanged) future. We want to draw upon our Human ingenuity to use the proverbial 'Ring' for good.

4 - Indigenous Perspectives on Apocalypse

In both Tolkien's work and our primary-world histories, indigenous and subaltern accounts provide important nuance to our narrativization of history. Kyle Powys White notes that, from an indigenous point of view, climate injustice and our present environmental crisis are "less about the spectre of a new future and more like the experience of *déjà vu*" (2017, 88). While the story of the Anthropocene positions 'apocalypse' as a future possibility, indigenous communities and people of colour have been subjected to countless apocalypses over the past 500 years, leading Kathryn Yusoff to argue that we must acknowledge either "a billion Black Anthropocenes or none" (2018, 17). She writes, "there is a need to question […] 'moves to innocence' - the claim that we failed to understand the violent repercussions of colonialism, industrialization, or capitalist modes of production and that these violences were an unforeseen by-product or excess of these practices and not a central tenet of them" (22). In Númenórean historiography, such a 'move to innocence' can be clearly seen in narrativizations of the *Atalantë* at the end of the Third Age, focusing predominantly on Sauron's manipulations and the transgression of divine law while entirely bypassing Númenor's long-standing involvement in the destruction of worlds.

From the perspectives of those the Númenóreans killed, enslaved, and exploited, one might say that there were countless 'Atalanti' throughout the Second Age – a key example of which is found in the incomplete tale of 'Tal-Elmar', concerning a tribe of Humans living in the Hills of Agar in the mid-to-late Second Age. While looking out on the sea, Tal-Elmar spots what he thinks to be "three strange birds" floating in the distance (*Peoples*, 426). His father, Hazad Longbeard, correctly identifies them as the perilous ships of the *Go-hilleg* (a local name for Númenórean colonists), warning his son:

> Greater than great houses are the ships of the *Go-hilleg*, and they bear store of men and goods, and yet are wafted by the winds […] they will send forth smaller boats laden with goods, and strange things both beautiful and useful such as our folk covet […] And if they do not return, men should be thankful. For if they come again it is in other guise. In greater numbers they come then: two ships or more together, stuffed with men and not goods […] they bear away evil booty, captives packed like beasts, the fairest women and children, or young men unblemished, and that is their end. (427)

Bearing warning of the potential danger to the local chieftain, Tal-Elmar is sent to converse with the ship-lords as an emissary. But after first being mistaken for one of the Eldar, he is ultimately captured and delivered to the Númenórean captain, who informs him, "your time of dwelling in these hills is come to an end. Here the men of the West have resolved to make their homes, and the folk of the dark must depart – or be slain" (437). This ultimatum is itself tantamount to a kind of *apocalypse*, highlighting the extent to which Númenóreans had already 'fallen' (in a moral sense) long before their watery cataclysm, and offering some important context for the later alignment of many so-called 'lesser Men' with Sauron's forces in his conflicts with the 'Men of the Sea' (*UT*, 282).

Not all indigenous perspectives on the *Atalantë* are centred around dispossession and death. In Tar-Aldarion's time, Númenor was a highly multicultural society: along with the peoples of Bëor, Haleth, and Hador, there were also many Drúedain living among the Númenóreans. The Drúedain warned Aldarion that his voyages to Middle-earth would lead to evil outcomes, but even though they were renowned for their wisdom and foresight, their counsel was ignored. As a result, they left Númenor and returned to the mainland, reporting that "the Great Isle no longer feels sure under our feet" (408). By the time of Ar-Pharazôn's rule, no Drúedain remained in Númenor, and while they long retained their autonomy in the mountains of Andrast, they ultimately fared poorly against Sauron's forces. By the end of the Third Age the Woses of Ghân-buri-Ghân were perhaps the last remaining Drúedanic society in Middle-earth, at which point it is evident that Orcs were not their only foes. In return for guiding Théoden and his men through the woods to Pelennor, Ghân's only request of the Rohirrim is that they "leave Wild Men alone in the woods and do not hunt them like beasts any more" (*RK*, 'The Ride of the Rohirrim,' 865).

Even amongst the Númenóreans, it is evident that the 'Faithful' in exile did not entirely abandon their colonial legacy. The establishment of the kingdoms of Gondor and Arnor was directly tied to the oppression and dispossession of indigenous communities like the Dunlendings, whose land was stolen by the Dúnedain and given to the Rohirrim (*RK*, 'Appendix A', 1101-2)

leading to long-standing bitterness and devastating consequences
. Perhaps if provided with a more faithful account of Númenor's
fall, the profound folly of such moves would have been more
apparent to the 'High Men' of the Third Age.

5 - Making Sense of a World's Ending

I argue that the profound tragedy of the Downfall of Númenor is
not the island's literal descent into the depths of the ocean, but
rather its moral 'fall' into oppressive paradigms of control and
the pursuit of permanence. The same might be said for our own
drowning world. Both the *Atalantë* and the Anthropocene are
stories about the cataclysmic changing of the Earth "in an hour
unlooked for by Men," but critical analysis reveals that both
were in fact long and complex processes rooted in a descent
from relational enchantment into patterns of oppression,
exploitation, and the pursuit of never-ending 'progress' (Curry
2023, 8-17). In both cases, societies that once maintained
close and respectful social relations 'fell' into chauvinism and
disregard, constructing contrived 'master identity' paradigms
that allowed them to justify the subjugation of all those they
deemed to be 'other.' Both processes began, in large part,
with the destruction of the so-called 'natural' world through
deforestation and ecocide, followed by the displacement,
dispossession, enslavement, and murder of indigenous peoples.
But in the end, historical perceptions of both processes were
whitewashed and recontextualised to support contemporary
ambitions – projecting culpability onto external scapegoats
while ignoring the responsibilities of the societies in question
in the perilous transformation of the world.

When engaged with critically stories like the 'Akallabêth'
can provide valuable clarity to our conceptualisations of our

own history. Storytelling is ultimately a world-making practice, and a powerful tool for "recovery," both in the sense of a "return and renewal of health" as well as the "regaining of a clear view" (*OFS*, 67-9). The stories that we tell ourselves about ourselves, and about our past and the world and beings around us, can have a profound impact on our values, experiences, and modes of engagement with the world. Myths are not merely explanatory, but also generative, directly contributing to the realities that we co-create. Tolkien once predicted that, "If men were ever in a state in which they did not want to know or could not perceive truth (facts or evidence), then Fantasy would languish until they were cured […] and become Morbid Delusion" (65). I would argue that many of our standard narratives of the so-called Anthropocene – including the reification of categories like 'Humanity' and 'nature,' the rejection of social context, and the notion that we have unexpectedly 'stumbled' into supreme agency and power – are precisely these kinds of tales. But not all myths are delusive, and it may be that so-called 'fantasy' holds the keys to both our destruction and our recovery, helping us imagine new ways of being in a more-than-Human world.

Storyteller David Novak suggests that stories about the end of the world – and indeed apocalypticism as an ontological worldview – arise not out of fears about an unknown future, but in fact "the deep resonant memory of the 'apocalypse' that has already happened." He proposes that "we are, in this time, already living in the post-apocalypse era […] we are the survivors […] our thousands of years of history is a long post-traumatic stress disorder" (2014). One might say that the very worlds that many of us inhabit are already post-apocalyptic in nature, and that our alienation from the living world is a primary trauma that still haunts our perception of reality. But rather than fight for a sustained *status quo* or lie in wait for the waves to swallow us up, what if we took this moment as an opportunity to imagine new ways of being? Neither Elendil nor Isildur could effectively 'save' Númenor from utter annihilation – but through the 'escape' of the Faithful, new life could emerge from the cracks of a crumbling world. Isildur could not stop Nimloth from being felled and burned on the dark altar, but he *was* able to salvage her last fruit so that a new sapling could grow in the future. The ending of one world is not the ending of *all* worlds – but it *is* an opportunity for us to consider which fruits are worth preserving on our path to 'recovery.'

Bibliography

Andersson, E. J., *Unseen Beings: How We Forgot the World is More Than Human,* (London: Hay House UK, 2023).

Bonneuil, C. and Fressoz, J., *The Shock of the Anthropocene: The Earth, History, and Us,* (London: Verso, 2015).

Colligs, B. M., 'The Forest as a Voice for Nature: Ecocritcism in Fantasy Literature,' in *Images of the Anthropocene in Speculative Fiction,* ed. by Tereza Dědinová, Weronika Łaszkiewicz, and Sylwia Borowska-Szerszun (London: Rowman & Littlefield Publishing Group, 2021), pp. 67-86.

Crosby, A., *Ecological Imperialism: The Biological Expansion of Europe, 900-1900,* (Cambridge: Cambridge University Press, 1986).

Curry, Patrick, *Defending Middle-Earth: Tolkien, Myth and Modernity* (New York: St. Martin's Press, 1997).
— 'Environmentalism and Eco-Criticism', in *J.R.R. Tolkien Encyclopedia: Scholarship and Critical Assessment,* ed. by M. D. C. Drout (New York: Routledge, 2013), p. 165.
— *Art and Enchantment: How Wonder Works,* (London: Routledge, 2023).

Hjulstad, Katrine L.A., 'The Tale of the Old Forest: The Damaging Effects of Forestry in J.R.R. Tolkien's Written Works,' *Journal of Tolkien Research,* 10.2, Article 7. (2020), <https://scholar.valpo.edu/journaloftolkienresearch/vol10/iss2/7>

Grove, J., 'Of an Apocalyptic Tone Recently Adopted in Everything: The Anthropocene or Peak Humanity?,' *Theory & Event,* 18.3 (2015), <https://www.muse.jhu.edu/article/586148>

Hynes, G., ''The Cedar is Fallen': Empire, Deforestation and the Fall of Númenor,' in *J.R.R. Tolkien: The Forest and the City*, ed. by Helen Conrad-O'Briain and Gerard Hynes (Portland, OR: Four Courts Press, 2013), pp. 123-132.

Latour, B., *Facing Gaia: Eight Lectures on the New Climatic Regime,* (Cambridge: Polity, 2017).

Le Guin, Ursula K., 'The Critics, the Monsters, and the Fantasists,' *The Wadsworth Circle,* 38.1/2 (2007).

Novak, David, *Chain of Arrows and the Shoulder of Giants*, online video recording, YouTube, 23 May 2014, <https://www.youtube.com/watch?v=ri5hspmAzmc> [accessed 10 June 2023].

Savransky, M., 'After Progress: Notes for an Ecology of Perhaps,' *Ephemera: Theory & Politics in Organization*, 21.1 (2021), pp. 267- 281.

Schneiderman, J., 'The Anthropocene Controversy,' in *Anthropocene Feminism*, ed. by Richard Grusin (Minneapolis, MN: University of Minnesota Press, 2017), pp. 170-189.

Scull, C. and Hammond, W. G., *The J.R.R. Tolkien Companion and Guide: Reader's Guide Part I: A-M,* (London: HarperCollins, 2017).

Siewers, A. K., 'Environmentalist Readings of Tolkien', in *J.R.R. Tolkien Encyclopedia: Scholarship and Critical Assessment*, ed. by M. D. C. Drout (New York: Routledge, 2013), pp. 166-67.

Tolkien, J.R.R., *The Silmarillion*, ed. by Christopher Tolkien (London: George Allen and Unwin, 1977).
— *The Lord of the Rings*, (London: George Allen and Unwin, 1984).
— *The Letters of J.R.R. Tolkien*, ed. by Humphrey Carpenter with the assistance of Christopher Tolkien (London: Harper Collins, 2006).
— *Tolkien On Fairy-Stories*, ed. by Verlyn Flieger and Douglas A. Anderson (London: HarperCollins, 2008).
— *The Lost Road and Other Writings*, ed. by Christopher Tolkien, three-volume deluxe edition (London: HarperCollins, 2017).
— *Sauron Defeated,* ed. by Christopher Tolkien, (London: HarperCollins, 2017).
— *Morgoth's Ring,* ed. by Christopher Tolkien, (London: HarperCollins, 2017).
— *The Peoples of Middle-earth*, ed. by Christopher Tolkien, (London: HarperCollins, 2017).
— *Unfinished Tales of Númenor and Middle-earth*, ed. by Christopher Tolkien, (London: HarperCollins, 2020).
— *The Nature of Middle-Earth*, ed. by Carl F. Hostetter (London: HarperCollins, 2021)
— *The Fall of Númenor and Other Tales from the Second Age of Middle-earth*, ed. by Brian Sibley (London: HarperCollins, 2022).

Whyte, K. P., 'Is it Colonial Dèja-Vu? Indigenous Peoples and Climate

Injustice,' in *Humanities for the Environment: Integrating Knowledge, Forming New Constellations of Practice*, ed. by Joni Adamson and Michael Davis (London: Routledge, 2017), pp. 88-105.

Williams, M., *Deforesting the Earth: From Prehistory to Global Crisis, An Abridgment,* (Chicago: The University of Chicago Press, 2006).

Woodhall, A., 'Addressing Anthropocentrism is Nonhuman Ethics: Evolution, morality, and nonhuman Beings' (unpublished thesis, University of Birmingham, 2016).

Monstrous (Im)mortality: Transhumanism and Ecocriticism in 'Akallabêth'

Kristine Larsen

1 - The Machine and the Transhuman

In 'On Fairy-stories' J.R.R. Tolkien names the avoidance of death the "oldest and deepest desire" (*OFS*, 74). Tolkien is not engaging in hyperbole here, as the quest for immortality is central to the oldest known epic, the Sumerian tale of Gilgamesh (Bostrom 2005, 1). Over the millennia, humanity has repeatedly turned to some external power – to technology – in its search for a means by which to subvert death (or at the very least defer old age for as long as possible). From the youth-restoring sea plant that Gilgamesh loses to the snake to the legendary fountain of youth, Dorian Gray's portrait to Victor Frankenstein's creation, humanity repeatedly appeals to technology to save it from the natural temporal failings of the flesh, and is too often sorely disappointed. In Tolkien's words, humanity "will rebel against the laws of the Creator – especially against mortality" which will "lead to the desire for Power […] and so to the Machine (or Magic)" (*Letters*, Letter 131, 145).

Patrick Curry reflects that in Tolkien's subcreation "any desperate attempt to 'conquer' death through magic not only fails but destroys life along the way" (2020, 24). For example, in a famous analogy Tolkien explained that the appointed lifespans of each of the intelligent species in his Secondary World "cannot really be *increased* qualitatively or quantitatively; so that prolongation in time is like […] 'spreading butter ever thinner' – it becomes an intolerable torment" (*Letters*, Letter 131, 155; emphasis original).

English evolutionary biologist and eugenicist Julian Huxley coined the term *transhumanism* in 1951 for the potential transcendence of the entire human species beyond its current nature (1968, 76). The term was afterwards adopted to describe the use of genetic engineering and computer technology (including artificial intelligence and cybernetics) to enhance humanity, a process that may eventually lead to the creation of a new posthuman species (Church and Regis 2012, 227). We can easily observe the seeds of transhumanism planted in the earliest science fiction, for example in Mary Shelley's *Frankenstein* (1818). Transhumanism embraces the rejection of the natural state of humanity in favor of technological enhancements; therefore, an ecocritical lens – investigating the relationship between humanity and the natural world – can be particularly useful in analyzing the limitations and pitfalls of transhumanist points of view. This paper investigates transhumanist themes and ecocritical lessons from the fall of the Númenóreans, especially as described in 'Akallabeth'.

2 - Tolkien and Early 20th Century Transhumanism

David B. Hogan and A. Mark Clarfield argue that *The Lord of the Rings* can be viewed as a response to the transhumanist and eugenicist agendas of such authors of J.B.S. Haldane and Olaf Stapledon (2007, 9). In *Daedalus or Science and the Future* (1924), Cambridge biochemist Haldane offers that once disease has been eradicated death will become similar to sleep. He argues that a "gentle decline into the grave at the end of a completed life's work" will conquer what he claims is a widespread "feeling that most lives are incomplete" (1924, 73), suggesting that we will accept our mortality once our lives are of some unnamed sufficient length.

Haldane's later essay 'The Last Judgement' focuses on how a species-level immortality might be achieved by outliving our planet. He includes a science fiction story in which anthropogenic technological changes to the environment force humanity to turn to technology to save it from its folly – genetic engineering of a new species of transhumans who can exist on Venus, which has likewise been artificially modified to meet their altered biological needs (Haldane 1930). Contrast this artificial, intentional evolution of humanity through technology to the natural evolution of the Hobbits as a species toward shorter average height as noted in *The Lord of the Rings* (*FR*, 'Prologue', 10-1). We may be tempted to draw a parallel with the humans of *Daedalus* who accept their extended yet limited lifespan with Aragorn, who, like a "good Númenórean died of free will when he felt it to be time to do so" (*Letters*, Letter 156, 205). He even offers to Arwen "now, therefore, I will sleep" (*RK*, 'Appendix A', 343). The important difference here is that Haldane's longeval transhumans still suffer a "gentle decline" whereas Aragorn releases his life after he "felt the approach of old age" but before he would "wither and fall" – there is no decline, gentle or otherwise (343).[1]

In *A Question of Time* (1997), Verlyn Flieger gives a detailed overview of the influence of engineer J.W. Dunne's 1927 work *An Experiment with Time* on Tolkien and C.S. Lewis as well as William Olaf Stapledon's *Last and First Men* (initially published in 1930 and highly influenced by Haldane's

---

1. Journee Cotton (2022) explores a problematic ableist and ageist side to Aragorn's motivation.

The Last Judgement) and *Last Men in London* (which appeared in 1932). Dunne posited the ability to travel in time within dreams, while Stapledon's fiction features time travel into the past and across the solar system through dreamlike trances. Stapledon's mythos follows the history of humanity over two billion years into the future, continually using genetic and planetary engineering to fight against natural disasters that threaten them with extinction. While the death of humanity as a whole is to be avoided at all cost, throughout *Last and First Men* Stapledon extols the virtues of accepting one's individual inevitable demise and warns against the foolishness of grasping at immortality (Stapledon 2007, 173, 208).

Lewis explained in a 1938 letter to Roger Lancelyn Green that he was motivated to write *Out of the Silent Planet* by Stapledon's *Last and First Men* and geneticist J.B.S. Haldane's collection of essays *Possible Worlds* (which contains 'The Last Judgement'), accusing both men of having the same "desperately immoral outlook" that he wrote into the Space Trilogy's corrupt scientist Weston (2004, 236). In the final novel in the 'Space' trilogy, *That Hideous Strength*, N.I.C.E. is dedicated to the "conquest of death", to break free from the "cocoon of organic life" and intentionally evolve humanity to the ultimate stage of existence, an immortal "artificial man, free from Nature" (Lewis 2003, 173-4). As will become clear later in this paper, in their efforts to utilize technology to change their human nature – to unnaturally extend their lives and, they hoped, eventually conquer death – the Númenóreans can be seen to parallel the end goal (although thankfully not the extreme corrupted ethics) of the scientists of N.I.C.E. In summary, all of these authors and their works – both those critical and supportive of transhumanism – were clearly within Tolkien's known influences.

3 - Ecocriticism and Power

Lewis's comment concerning an "artificial man, free from Nature" is particularly interesting. In *Ecocriticism and the Idea of Culture*, Helena Feder reflects that our embrace of extreme technological innovations, such as those adopted by transhumanism, can be read as a response to "culture's terror of nature's agency" (2014, 73). This concept of "nature's agency" is central to Tolkien's works (Roman 2015, 97). This inherent power in nature complicates the relationship between Man and Nature in Middle-earth, because, as Tolkien himself warned, "'power' is an ominous and sinister word in all these tales" (*Letters*, Letter 131, 152). Feder further explains that "the drive for technological innovation may be seen as an extension of or reaction to this horror" at nature's power, and warns that while attempts to control nature through technology try to "keep entropy at bay, it may also become its servant" (2018, 8). In other words, technological attempts to thwart decline, disorder, and death may actually hasten it in the end.

Ecocriticism of the Númenóreans (e.g., Dickerson and Evans 2011; Hjulstad 2020) often focuses on the mass deforestation of Middle-earth blamed on their fleet building, most notably as referenced in the c.1965 essay 'The Port of Lond Daer' ('Appendix D' of 'The History of Galadriel and Celeborn' in *Unfinished Tales*) and 'Dwarves and Men' (late 1969 or later; published in *The Peoples of Middle-earth*). The first essay blames the loss of the then vast forests of Middle-earth's coastlines on the Mariner-king Tar-Aldarion and his "great hunger for timber, desiring to make Númenor into a great naval power" (*UT*, 262). According to this version of the history, the indigenous residents of Middle-earth only became hostile towards the Númenóreans after their "tree-felling became devastating"; in response, the Númenóreans "became ruthless in their fellings, giving no thought to husbandry or replanting" (262). Over time, the "devastation wrought by the Númenóreans was incalculable" because the majority of their lumber is said to have come from Middle-earth (262-3).

'Dwarves and Men' tells a similar tale of the forest-dwellers in Middle-earth who came to see the Númenóreans as enemies "because of their ruthless treatment and their devastation of the forests" (*Peoples*, 314). In his commentary to the essay, Christopher Tolkien confirms that the desire of the Númenóreans to create large navies led them to become "reckless" in their harvesting of trees (329). But a close reading of the c.1965 'Aldarion and Erendis: The Mariner's Wife' (*Unfinished Tales*) reveals that this was not always the case. As Katrine L. Hjulstad points out, for his part Aldarion engages in "sustainable forestry" so that his ship building would not have been the cause of "massive deforestation" (2020, 11). Indeed, Aldarion is described as intentionally planting trees on numerous occasions (e.g., *UT*, 182, 190). The problem comes about six centuries later, when Tar-Ciryatan, the twelfth ruler of the island nation, comes to throne, builds great fleets and engages in oppressive occupation and colonialization policies (221). This in turn ultimately leads to the mass deforestation, a combination of what Hjulstad describes as a greatly enhanced need for wood paired with a lack of a policy of "sustainable forestry. […] While Aldarion was not the cause of the destruction, the works he began were," as trees were increasingly seen merely as the tool of technology (2020, 11-2). This abuse of nature is one important step along the Númenóreans' downward path to transhumanism and the utter rejection of their biological nature.

4 - Deforestation and Transhumanism: The Rejection of Nature

Hugh Keenan notes that at the end of the Third Age the destruction of the forests led to the demise of not only the land but its habitants. It is therefore important to note that the "return of the forests to Isengard and to the Shire signals the return of life to dead and dying lands (2000, 11). Dickerson and Evans similarly highlight this connection of "deforestation with 'dead and dying lands'" (2011, 134). Again, while ecocriticism of the Númenóreans often focusses on their later policy of mass deforestation in the service of technology (ship-building), in their subsequent open rejection of their mortal nature they succumbed to a vain transhumanist lust for physical immortality, denying their natural state, and embracing technology in the form of ungodly alchemical experiments in which "their wise men laboured unceasingly" (*Silmarillion*, 266).

While this fall happened over many centuries, the seeds were planted from the initial days of the island. The c.1965 essay 'Lives of the Númenóreans', published in *The Nature of Middle-earth*, explains that the Edain had asked for only two things from the Valar in acknowledgement of their part in the downfall of Morgoth: "long life and Peace" (*Nature*, 316). There is an inherent irony in this request, because *peace* can be interpreted in two very different ways – a military peace (which the Valar granted, for a time, with the defeat of Morgoth) and the peace that ultimately proved more elusive, an inner peace derived from accepting their mortality.[2] For while the same

---

2. One might argue that the Númenóreans themselves are transhumans, although there are two very important differences: first, there was no change in their ultimate nature (they remained mortal) and the change was accomplished through the grace of Ilúvatar – through divine intervention –

essay notes that Elros died about age 500, most Númenóreans were given lifespans closer to 400 years (317). To be sure, four centuries is a lengthy lifespan, but it is finite.

Tolkien is careful to explain that the unnatural "clinging to life" (refusing to voluntarily accept the Gift of Ilúvatar at the appropriate time) was "brought about by the Shadow and the rebellion of the Númenóreans" and was first seen only in the fourteenth generation, after the death of Tar-Ciryatan's son (317). It is important to note that this rejection of their biological nature and a hunger for more life came *after* a similar economic and political shift from trade and exploration to exploitation: they first sought power over the natural environment and then over their very physical nature. I therefore suggest that the ordered connection between degraded environment in terms of deforestation and unnatural rejection of death is not accidental but symptomatic of their overall fall. As Dickerson and Evans describe, the fall is driven by the Númenóreans' loss of respect for the gifts of the Valar, including their island itself, and a shift towards exploitation; they were no longer content to be as men but sought to be as gods (2011, 61-2). This is coupled with a loss of respect for the expanded lifespan they had already been granted, and the Gift of Ilúvatar in general, the ability to leave the world, unlike Elves and the Valar who are bound to it until its uncertain end.

Tolkien's language in 'Akallabêth' is very precise in this regard:

> Now this *yearning* grew ever greater with the years; and the Númenóreans began to *hunger* for the undying city that they saw from afar, and the desire of everlasting life, to escape from

---

and not through technology.

death and the ending of delight, grew strong upon them; and as their power and glory grew greater their *unquiet* increased. (*Silmarillion*, 263-4; emphasis mine)

We observe that they suffer with *yearning, hunger, desire*, and unquiet, which their increased power only seems to exacerbate – recall Feder's warning that attempts to control nature through technology may instead lead to an increase of entropy or disorder (2018, 8). But rather than recognize the self-destructive nature of the path they have embarked on, the Númenóreans instead increase their unnatural embrace of technology, especially in the service of achieving transhumanism – of going beyond their human nature. Further on in 'Akallabêth' we read

But the *fear* of death grew ever darker upon them, and they *delayed* it by all means that they could; and they began to *build* great houses for their dead, while their wise men *laboured unceasingly* to discover if they might the secret of recalling life, or at the least of the *prolonging* of Men's days. Yet they achieved only the art of *preserving* incorrupt the dead flesh of Men. (*Silmarillion*, 266; emphasis mine)

Again, certain action words associated with technology stand out, including *delayed, build, laboured unceasingly, prolonging, preserving*, all set into motion by fear. There is a sense of desperation here, of futility, of wheels spinning but getting nowhere, a less successful version of Saruman's mind of "metal and wheels" (*TT*, 'Treebeard', 76).

Dickerson and Evans remind us that in Tolkien's Secondary World "symbolism of moral and ethical failure involves images of death and destruction of the natural world" for example the fate of Nimloth, the White Tree of Númenor. As a descendent of one of the Two Trees of Valinor, Nimloth is "mythically symbolic of the whole realm of nature and the life within it" (Dickerson and Evans 2011, 62). Therefore, the waning interest in and respect to the tree paid by the Númenóreans is evidence of the increasing evil infecting their culture. A momentary pause in the steady moral decline of his people is seen in the reign of Tar-Palantir, who carefully tended the precious tree, notably pronouncing that the end of the line of the Kings would come with the death of the tree (*Silmarillion*, 269).

It is therefore not unexpected (but deeply symbolic) when Sauron urges Ar-Pharazôn to finally cut down the tree, its destruction is an undeniable and irrevocable sign of the Númenóreans' rebuke of their relationship with the Blessed Lands and with it, a rejection of the Gift of Ilúvatar and their mortal nature. Ar-Pharazôn clearly understands the weight of what is asked of him, and only relents after Isildur steals a fruit from the White Tree. The language used in this scene is precise: "the King yielded to Sauron and felled the White Tree", ominous terminology given the history of deforestation by the Númenóreans (*Silmarillion*, 273). Whether it was felled directly by his hand or his order is not clear, but in either case Ar-Pharazôn is clearly responsible for the tree's intended demise. The physical fate of Nimloth is far more lamentable than that of the trees felled to make ships or other items that the Númenóreans used in their daily lives; instead, it fueled the first ritual fire that Sauron burned in his new temple to Melkor, Armenelos the Golden. Nimloth was but the first living thing sacrificed to fuel the offering fires made by men in the hope that Melkor "should release them from Death" (273). Instead, it ultimately leads to the death of Númenor, and in time all of the gifts granted to the Númenóreans.

5 - Degeneration and the Númenóreans

Tolkien recognizes in one of his author's notes to the philosophical debate 'Athrabeth Finrod ah Andreth' that the 'Tale of Adanel' – the story of humanity's early decline into Melkor worship – has significant parallels to 'Akallabêth' (*Morgoth*, 344). Tolkien is clear about the reason for the initial fall of humanity in Middle-earth – they desired to acquire knowledge too quickly, openly disobeying the limits set upon them by their creator, Ilúvatar. According to the legend, the punishment meted out for this disobedience was either the beginning of their mortality, or a great shortening of their lifespans. In either case we see a deep-rooted tradition among humans denying their current mortal lifespans to be their true nature. As such, it provides a justification for trying to 'fix' the problem through knowledge and technology. A second fall related to mortality is that recounted in 'Akallabêth', where, as Dimitra Fimi points out, the lifespan of the Númenóreans begins to diminish when they seek unnatural immortality, a "sign of the withdrawal of the favour of the Valar" (2010, 148). In 'Appendix A' of *The Lord of the Rings* it is explained that Tar-Atanamir, son of the great ship-builder (and deforester) Tar-Ciryatan, was the first king to claim he had a right to the supposed immortality of the Eldar (*RK*, 'Appendix A', 316). The royal house and their followers became "estranged from the Eldar and the Valar" (*RK*, 'Appendix A', 316). Again, the essay 'Lives of the Númenóreans' confirms this, as previously noted explaining how the unnatural "clinging to life" by the Númenóreans is concomitant with a contraction of their average lifespan after the fourteenth generation (*Nature*, 317).

Tolkien makes the point that while their "power and wealth" increased "their years lessened as their fear of death grew" (*RK*,

'Appendix A', 316). As previously noted from *The Silmarillion*, they turned to technology in the hopes of not only reversing the trend, but to further expand their lifespans beyond what previous generations had enjoyed, but to no avail. The same was true of the desperate attempt to sacrifice to Melkor; indeed, it resulted in even further reduction of the lifespans of many, as death "came sooner and more often" (*Silmarillion*, 274). Previously men had aged slowly and "laid them down in the end to sleep, when they were weary at last of the world" (this description admittedly sounding similar to the transhumans of Haldane's *Daedalus*); in contrast "now madness and sickness availed them" and they were fearful of death (274).[3]

The third fall of the Númenóreans, specifically of the descendants of the Faithful who escaped the destruction of the island and had for so long remained true to the Valar and to their nature, predictably came at last, beginning with Isildur's claiming of the One Ring from Sauron's hand. As Faramir painfully explains to Frodo of his ancestors in Gondor

> Death was ever present, because the Númenóreans still, as they had in their old kingdom, and so lost it, hungered after endless life unchanging. [...] Childless lords sat in aged halls musing on heraldry; in secret chambers withered men compounded strong elixirs, or in high cold towers asked questions of the stars. And the last king in the line of Anárion had no heir. (*TT*, 'The Window on the West', 286)

---

3. A discussion of ageism and ableism (which have clear connections to the transhumanism movement) and the fall of the Númenóreans is beyond the scope of this paper. The interested reader is directed to Cotton (2022) and Hogan and Clarfield (2007) for relevant background material and discussion.

There is a notable decrease in their nobility, and apparently even their fertility. Yet still they cling to technology, the false god that failed them, as it had their ancestors, and their ancestors before them. Similarly, at the Council of Elrond, the elf lord recounts how after the Last Alliance of Elves and Men "the race of Númenor has decayed" and their lifespan decreased (*FR*, 'The Council of Elrond', 257).

Dimitra Fimi points out that in Middle-earth the dwindling lifespan of the descendants of the Númenóreans is due, at least in part, to a "'decay' of their 'blood'" when it is combined with "that of 'lesser men'" (2010, 148). Such an evolutionary decline in humans due to their fall from their original Edenic state of perfection is termed *degeneration* in theological discussions (Walter 1956, 422). The middle of the 19th century saw a pseudo-scientific application of the concept, in concert with a Lamarckian model of evolution. In his *Treatise on the Degeneration of the Human Species* (1857), French psychiatrist Bénédict Augustin Morel argued that mental degradation of individuals caused by an environment steeped in poverty, alcoholism, and pollution would be passed down to their children, causing increased degeneracy leading to sterility by the fourth generation (Hurley 1996, 66). Degeneration was thus viewed as a kind of reverse evolution, as evolution was often erroneously depicted as the upward directed, linear march of life from more primitive (and hence less 'fit') toward more complex (and, it was reasoned, more 'fit') forms, especially in the case of humans. Taken in sum, humanity in Middle-earth – at least those originally considered the most noble or ethically the 'most fit' – have ironically fallen or degenerated the farthest, in three separate 'falls', as described in 'The Tale of Adanel', 'Akallabêth', and Faramir's conversation with Frodo (describing the further fall of the Númenórean exiles in Gondor). In each of these cases the fall is fueled by humanity openly rejecting their nature – their natural state – and attempting to become 'more' – to become transhuman – through forbidden knowledge and technology.

6 - The Fantasist and the Realist

Transhumanist philosopher Nick Bostrom, Director of the Oxford University Future of Humanity Institute, argues that there exists a "tendency in at least some individuals to always search for a way around every obstacle and limitation to human life and happiness" (2005, 1). This is certainly true of the humans in Middle-earth. However, Tolkien is quite clear in the intended lesson from the repeated failure of the Edain's rejection of their natural state and futile attempts at transhumanism. As he famously reflected in a 1944 letter to his son Christopher

> There is the tragedy and despair of all machinery laid bare. [...] Labour-saving machinery only creates endless and worse labour. And in addition to this fundamental disability of a creature, is added the Fall, which makes our devices not only fail of their desire but turn to new and horrible evil. (*Letters*, Letter 75, 87-8)

Tolkien adds that this leads "inevitably from Daedalus and Icarus to the Giant Bomber" although in this case perhaps we should say from *Daedalus or Science and the Future* to 'Akallabêth', or from the Edain to entropy.

Patrick Curry reflects that transhumanists are "terrified of death, so their ultimate ideal also requires replacing organic parts with sophisticated technology [...] The result, we are assured, turns mere humans into immortal cyborgs" (2020, 23). But this comes only at the utter rejection of our basic organic human nature, a cost that Tolkien clearly argues is both foolhardy and morally bankrupt. As Curry thoughtfully ends his essay, "*who here is the fantasist, and who is the realist?*" (24; emphasis original).

Bibliography

Bostrom, Nick, 'A History of Transhumanist Thought', *Journal of Evolution and Technology*, 14.1 (2005), pp. 1-25.

Church, George, and Ed Regis, *Regenesis: How Synthetic Biology Will Reinvent Nature and Ourselves*, (New York: Basic Books, 2012).

Cotton, Journee, 'An Environmental Bioethical Approach to Ageing Bodies of Middle-earth: Ableism and Fertility', *Oxonmoot 2002*, Oxford, UK, 3 September 2022.

Curry, Patrick, 'Fantasy in Transhumanism and Tolkien', *The Ecological Citizen*, 4.1 (2020), pp. 23-24.

Dickerson, Matthew, and Jonathan Evans, *Ents, Elves, and Eriador: The Environmental Vision of J.R.R. Tolkien*, (Lexington: The University of Kentucky Press, 2011).

Dunne. J.W., *An Experiment with Time*, 3rd ed., (London: Faber and Faber Limited, 1934).

Feder, Helena, *Ecocriticism and the Idea of Culture: Biology and the Bildungsroman*, (Surrey: Routledge, 2014).
— 'Transhumanism, Frankenstein, and Extinction', *Litteraria Pragensia*, 28.56 (2018), pp. 7-18.

Fimi, Dimitra, *Tolkien, Race and Cultural History*, (New York: Palgrave Macmillan, 2010).

Flieger, Verlyn, *A Question of Time: J. R. R. Tolkien's Road to Faërie*, (Kent: Kent University Press, 1997).

Haldane, J.B.S., *Daedalus or Science and the Future*, (New York: E.P. Dutton and Company, 1924).
— *Possible Worlds and Other Essays*, (London: Chatto and Windus, 1930).

Hjulstad, Katrine L., 'The Tale of the Old Forest: The Damaging Effects of Forestry in J.R.R. Tolkien's Written Works', *Journal of Tolkien Research*, 10.2 (2020), article 7, <https://scholar.valpo.edu/journaloftolkienresearch/vol10/iss2/7/> [accessed 7 June 2023].

Hogan, David B., and A. Mark Clarfield, 'Venerable or Vulnerable: Ageing and Old Age in J.R.R. Tolkien's *The Lord of the Rings*', *Medical Humanities*, 33 (2007), pp. 5-10.

Hurley, Kelly, *The Gothic Body: Sexuality, Materialism, and Degeneration at the Fin De Siècle*, (Cambridge: Cambridge University Press, 1996).

Huxley, Julian, 'Transhumanism', *Journal of Humanistic Psychology*, 8.1 (1968), pp. 73-76.

Jeffers, Susan, *Arda Inhabited: Environmental Relationships in The Lord of the Rings*, (Kent: Kent State University Press, 2014).

Keenan, Hugh T., 'The Appeal of *The Lord of the Rings*: A Struggle for Life', in *J.R.R. Tolkien's The Lord of the Rings*, ed. by Harold Bloom, (Philadelphia: Chelsea House Publishers), pp. 3-15.

Lewis, C.S., *That Hideous Strength*, (New York: Simon and Schuster, 2003).
— *The Collected Letters of C.S. Lewis, vol. 2*, ed. by Walter Hooper, (San Francisco: Harper 2004).

Roman, Christopher, 'Thinking with the Elements: J.R.R. Tolkien's Ecology and Object-Oriented Ontology', in *Representations of Nature in Middle-earth*, ed. by Martin Simonsen, (Zurich and Jena: Walking Tree Publishers, Zurich and Jena, 2015), pp. 95-118.

Stapledon, W. Olaf, *Last and First Men*, (Oxford: Benediction Classics, 2007).
— *Last Men in London*, (Oxford: Oxford City Press, 2009).

Tolkien, J.R.R., *Unfinished Tales of Númenor and Middle-earth*, ed. by Christopher Tolkien, (Boston: Houghton Mifflin, 1980).
— *The Fellowship of the Ring*, (Boston: Houghton Mifflin, 1993).
— *Morgoth's Ring*, ed. by Christopher Tolkien, (Boston: Houghton Mifflin, 1993).
— *The Return of the King*, (Boston: Houghton Mifflin, 1993).
— *The Two Towers*, (Boston: Houghton Mifflin, 1993).
— *The Peoples of Middle-earth*, ed. by Christopher Tolkien, (Boston: Houghton Mifflin, 1996).
— *The Letters of J.R.R. Tolkien*, ed. by Humphrey Carpenter with the assistance of Christopher Tolkien, (Boston: Houghton Mifflin, 2000).

— *The Silmarillion*, ed. by Christopher Tolkien, (Boston: Houghton Mifflin, 2001).
— *Tolkien on Fairy-stories*, ed. by Verlyn Flieger and Douglas A. Anderson, (London: HarperCollins, 2008).
— *The Nature of Middle-earth*, ed. by Carl Hostetter, (Boston: Houghton Mifflin Harcourt, 2021).
Walter, Richard D., 'What Became of the Degenerate? A Brief History of a Concept', *Journal of the History of Medicine and Allied Sciences*, 11.4 (1956), pp. 422-429.

"By the Waters of Anduin We Lay Down and Wept": Exilic Theology in the 'Akallabêth'

Rev. Tom Emanuel

An exemplary nation is elected by God to fulfill a unique calling. Summoned to a promised land of material and spiritual abundance and tutored in the ways of wisdom, God's chosen people grow in power and splendor. Soon, however, cracks begin to form: their leaders fall away from their covenant to love God and love their neighbors. The radical vision upon which the community was founded erodes, to be replaced with oppression of the poor and elite entanglement in webs of imperial power. At the apex of its hubris, the nation is laid low by a cataclysm so total that it shatters the people's understanding of themselves, their world, and their God. A handful of survivors are subsequently forced into exile. Looking back from a distant land, the faithful attempt to come to terms with the enormity of the catastrophe. The question looms like a storm-cloud filling the horizon: *how could God allow this to happen?*

Adherents of the Abrahamic faiths will instantly recognize this as the story of Israel in the period leading up to and immediately following the destruction of Jerusalem by the Babylonian Empire in 586 BCE. Fans of J.R.R. Tolkien's literary mythology may notice that it is also the Downfall of Númenor. In this paper I wish to tease out the parallels between these two mythic narratives of fidelity, apostasy, and catastrophe. I will read the exilic Prophet Jeremiah in conversation with Tolkien's 'Akallabêth' and the figure to whom its authorship is attributed within Tolkien's secondary world: Elendil the Faithful, leader of the Númenóreans in exile. Jeremiah and the 'Akallabêth' both address the problem of theodicy, the question of how an all-powerful, all-loving God can permit suffering and evil. Their twinned approaches to this conundrum shed light on the theological dynamics at work, not only in Tolkien's fiction, but also in his (and our) primary world. I close by suggesting that Tolkien's legendarium as a whole can be read as theodicy, a mythopoetic reckoning with the irrevocable loss of a communal past and the challenge of living into a hopeful future in a broken world.

To note the parallels between Tolkien's myth of Númenor and Plato's myth of Atlantis is to run the risk of restating the obvious. Tolkien repeatedly and explicitly links Númenor with his "Atlantis-haunting," his Dream of the Great Wave (*Letters*, Letter 257, 347). Verlyn Flieger has shown that he also draws in Celtic legends of drowned western lands such as Lyonesse off the coast of Cornwall and Hy-Brasil off the coast of Ireland (2017, 217). Elsewhere Tolkien links Númenor with the Biblical Flood, calling Elendil "a Noachian figure" (*Letters*, Letter 131, 156) and compares it to ancient Mediterranean civilizations including Rome (*Letters*, Letter 294, 376), Byzantium (*Letters*, Letter 131, 157), and especially Egypt (*Letters*, Letter 211, 281). Pamina Fernández Camacho has explored the island kingdom's wider Near Eastern connections, including Adûnaic's debt to Semitic languages (2016, 203-4) and Númenor's maritime empire which can be likened to the ancient Phoenicians and Carthaginians (2023, 85). She also draws parallels between the 'Akallabêth' and the biblical Exodus (2016, 204). Caryn Cooper and Kevin Whetter follow suit, noting the similarity between Ar-Pharazôn the last King of Númenor and the oppressive

Pharaoh of Exodus, right down to their names (2020, 3-4), as well as the way in which the 'Akallabêth' functions as the "founding narrative of the Dúnedain of Middle-earth" in much the same way that Exodus does for Israel (2). However, whereas the Exodus narrates God's liberating activity in the history of the Hebrew people, the Downfall of Númenor tells the story of a divinely-wrought catastrophe. When Megan Fontenot reads Númenor through the lens of apocalypse, she strikes nearer to the scriptural mark (2019, 92-3). But for all their portrayal of cosmic devastation, Jewish and Christian apocalypses are fundamentally eucatastrophic: the apocalyptic 'unveiling' is a harsh but necessary prelude to the hopeful revelation of the Reign of God. The Fall of Númenor, meanwhile, is an all-but-unmitigated disaster.

If we seek a biblical prototype for the 'Akallabêth', the exilic prophet Jeremiah is a better fit than Exodus, Revelation, or even Noah's Flood. Jeremiah's prophetic career begins during the reign of King Josiah of Judah in 626 BCE, spanning the destruction of Jerusalem by the Babylonians in 586 BCE and the subsequent exile of a significant portion of the Judean population. According to the royal theology of Judah's ruling elites, "because [YHWH][1] had chosen the Davidic dynasty, neither it nor its capital, Jerusalem, could ever be destroyed. The visible sign of this guarantee was the Temple, [YHWH]'s

---

[1]. I render the name of the God of Israel here and elsewhere as YHWH, which according to Jewish tradition cannot be pronounced and which is traced back etymologically to the Hebrew root H-Y-H "to be, to become." Compare this to God's self-revelation to Moses in the Burning Bush: *eyeh asher eyeh*, "I Am Who I Am" (Exodus 3:14). The Name of God is not spoken on the grounds that it *cannot* be spoken; *Adonai* "the Lord" and *Hashem* "the Name" are two common glosses in liturgical and everyday speech, respectively. Many modern scholars use the vocalized form "Yahweh" to designate the ancient Israelite deity; I follow the rabbinical tradition.

own home" (Coogan and Chapman 2016, 307). By way of contrast, Jeremiah proclaims that the people must constantly renew their covenant commitments to love God (Deut. 6:4-5) and love their neighbors as themselves (Lev. 19:18) if they wish to remain in the Promised Land. The Judeans have fallen away from their holy vocation to do justice and seek peace, but Jeremiah promises on God's behalf:

[I]f you truly amend your ways and your doings, if you truly act justly one with another, if you do not oppress the alien, the orphan, and the widow or shed innocent blood in this place, and if you do not go after other gods to your own hurt, then I will dwell with you in this place, in the land that I gave to your ancestors forever and ever. (Jer. 7:5-7)[2]

By the early decades of the sixth century BCE, however, Judah has entered into strategic alliances with regional imperial powers in a doomed campaign to stave off the might of Babylon, funneling resources into military armament rather than care for the vulnerable (Coogan and Chapman 2016, 295-7). Babylon's response is to invade Judah, raze Jerusalem to the ground, and send its inhabitants into exile. Jeremiah's own career concludes in Egypt, where he prophesies the eventual restoration of the fortunes of Judah and a return to the Holy Land (cf. Jer. 31:9-11). The Book of Jeremiah is presented as a collection of the sayings of the prophet, compiled by his scribe Baruch (Jer. 36:4), but the actual history of its composition is more complicated. It appears to have been assembled in pieces over the course of the mid-sixth century BCE, reaching its final form during or immediately following the Babylonian

---

2. All Bible quotations are taken from the New Revised Standard Version Updated Edition (NRSVUE).

Exile (Coogan and Chapman 2016, 301-2). As Old Testament scholar Kathleen O'Connor writes, "what the book of Jeremiah does is to present a portrait of the prophet that mixes fact and interpretation inextricably. [...] Its purpose was to help the people make sense of their tragedy, recover their identity, and move toward the future" (1998, 178).

Before I can argue that the 'Akallabêth' fulfills a similar purpose for the Númenórean exiles, I must first sketch out the complicated genesis of the narrative. The composition of the Númenor-myth falls out into three major periods: (a) the 'Fall of Númenor,' written in conjunction with *The Lost Road* in and around 1936; (b) the 'Drowning of Anadûnê,' which emerged alongside *The Notion-Club Papers* in 1944; and (c) the 'Akallabêth', which was completed in the late 1950s and which Christopher Tolkien published largely (but not entirely) intact in *The Silmarillion* in 1977 (Flieger 2017, 160). According to Christopher Tolkien, these three versions of the legend represent three different textual "traditions" within Middle-earth: the Elvish "Fall," the Mannish "Drowning," and the mixed Dúnedanic 'Akallabêth' (*Sauron*, 406-7). He is here referring to his father's elaborate metatextual conceit that every story of Middle-earth is "actually" written by a particular character in Middle-earth. Every text embodies a particular, limited viewpoint, informed by the fictional narrator's cultural and historical situation (cf. Flieger 2005, xiv). Regarding the 'Akallabêth' specifically, the 'Line of Elros,' also written in the late 1950s and published in *Unfinished Tales*, attributes it to Elendil and notes that copies of the text were preserved in Gondor (*UT*, 227).

There are good textual reasons for accepting Elendil's authorship in this sense. One is the narrative prominence and detail of conversations between Elendil and his father Amandil.

Such private information could only have come from Elendil himself after his father's departure to the West (*Silmarillion*, 275-6). Likewise, the critical moment of the Downfall itself is narrated from Elendil's emotional perspective in his ship off the eastern coast of Númenor (279-80). However, the final paragraphs of the published 'Akallabêth' are clearly the additions of a later commentator, with their reference to the changed shape of the world and latter-day legends of figures like Ælfwine of England who stumbled upon the Straight Road to Elvenhome (281-2). In fact, in a frame narrative which Christopher Tolkien excised from the published text, the 'Akallabêth' is presented as direct address to Ælfwine from an unnamed narrator in Tol Eressëa, presumably the Elvish historian Pengoloð (*Peoples*, 141-3, 159). If we accept the metafictional frame, Pengoloð must have had access to a copy of the 'Akallabêth' which was brought over the Sundering Seas by one of the returning Elvish exiles, perhaps Elrond himself. I proceed upon the assumption that while the final text of the 'Akallabêth' must have passed through the editorial hands of both scribes of Gondor as well as the Eldar of the Lonely Isle, its core originates with Elendil himself.

This sets us up to discern the theological work that the 'Akallabêth' is doing for the exiled Númenóreans. For the Hebrew prophets, God is in control of history: everything that occurs is ultimately of God's will (Coogan 2008, 86). For Jeremiah, the destruction of Jerusalem is no senseless tragedy; rather, God has used the Babylonian Empire to punish unfaithful Judah. The demolition of the Temple, previously believed to be God's dwelling-place on earth, thus produces a radical transformation in Israelite theology. The prophets herald the shift from henotheism, belief in multiple gods but with primary commitment to a single deity, to monotheism, belief in a single transcendent deity (42). However, monotheism produces a conundrum which will be familiar to modern believers and nonbelievers alike: if God is indeed the omnipotent Lord of History, why does God fail to prevent suffering and evil? This is the problem of theodicy. Jeremiah provides one answer: suffering is deserved punishment for wrongdoing. This theodicy of "blessings and curses" is not the only biblical response to the problem of pain, as the book of Job proves, but it remains a powerful strain in the theological heritage of the Abrahamic faiths. Christian process theologian Catherine Keller views it as an understandable but nevertheless misguided attempt to maintain God's omnipotence at the expense of God's mercy; divine love must be sacrificed upon the altar of divine control (2007, 81).

The 'Akallabêth' articulates a fundamentally similar theodicy in response to a fundamentally similar catastrophe, a fact which Elendil's authorship brings into focus. The capsule history of Númenor which comprises the first section of the text provides a theological genealogy of Ilúvatar's role in Númenórean history. The Dúnedain receive the land of Númenor as a reward for their role in the war against Morgoth in the First Age. The price of this gift is continued faithfulness to Ilúvatar and to the Valar as his plenipotentiaries. But for Elendil and the latter-day Númenóreans, the existence of Ilúvatar is a matter of belief, whereas mortality, the so-called 'Gift of Ilúvatar,' is an inescapable reality. Sauron exploits the felt distance between the invisibility of God and the visibility of Death to build support for his idolatrous cult of Melkor, telling Ar-Pharazôn that "the Valar have deceived you concerning him, putting forward the name of Eru, a phantom devised in the folly of their hearts, seeking to enchain Men in servitude to themselves" (*Silmarillion*, 272). Elendil and his followers remain unconvinced, and with prophetic insight foresee that the time is coming when Númenor's pursuit of deathlessness will turn to its undoing (cf. Heschel 2001, 15). Unlike readers who can take Tolkien's own pronouncements about the metaphysics of Middle-earth at face value, however, the Faithful have no guarantees. Ilúvatar's existence and the true nature of mortality must be taken on, well, *faith*.

Thus, when the disaster comes to pass, Elendil and his followers do not and cannot have direct knowledge of the mind of Ilúvatar. The information we find in the published 'Akallabêth', recounting the words and deeds of Ar-Pharazôn in Valinor and explaining the Valar's motivations in yielding up the government of Arda (*Silmarillion*, 278-9), must derive from either from Elvish sources in Tol Eressëa or, if they do originate with Elendil, surmise. Once in Middle-earth, Elendil simply cannot have absolute certainty about why the Downfall happened. Instead, he is left with the inescapable, shattering fact that it *did* happen. I read the 'Akallabêth' as Elendil coming to terms with the enormity of that fact, the loss of the land he loved and the deaths of untold numbers of his countryfolk – including, we must not forget, the children and non-human inhabitants of Númenor, all of whom have now paid the price for the sins of others. A theodicy of divine punishment for apostasy is perfectly comprehensible given the circumstances, but it generates the same problems as the blessings and curses of Jeremiah. Is a God who actively wills the slaughter of the innocents a God worth believing in?

This is not an idle question about the motivations of a fictional narrator; Tolkien's entire mythopoetic project can be understood as theodicy, a response to the collapse of meaning in the face of untold human suffering during the twentieth century. One need only look to the First World War in which

Tolkien himself served. "Something has gone crack," he wrote upon the death of his friend Rob Gilson at the Somme in 1916 (qtd. in Garth 2003, 169). In one sentence he captures the feeling that pervaded his generation and, in some ways, all the generations who were to follow them. Charles Taylor points to World War I as the critical inflection point in the decline of religious belief in the modern West. The industrial 'progress' of the Western colonial powers in modernity had not produced a secular utopia, still less the Heavenly City on earth. Its chief outcome was rather the disenchantment of the world, the immiseration of the masses, and a military conflagration of unprecedented proportions whose perfunctory conclusion set the stage for two decades of economic collapse and another, even bloodier war. Taylor asks: "how to respond to *this* sense, the idea that we are living after the demise of a viable order? […] [T]he sense of living in a shattered order has remained at some level as a truth of experience" (2020, 408-9). The God who could permit such senseless violence was—is—simply no longer credible to many people, perhaps especially those like Tolkien who served on the front lines and witnessed the pointless slaughter of their friends and countrymen.

Tolkien, famously, did not abandon his Roman Catholicism. But given his identification with the dreamer-protagonists of *The Lost Road* and *The Notion Club Papers*, and given the identification of those dreamer-protagonists with Elendil, it seems reasonable to suggest that Elendil is a figure with whom Tolkien felt a special kinship. Like him, and like the Prophet Jeremiah, Tolkien was a devout believer who was forced by unendurable circumstances to square his belief in a good and just God with an evil and unjust world. The exercise of parsing Elendil's 'Akallabêth' as a text produced by a historically situated individual with his own theological leanings and longings can help us to read Tolkien's 'Akallabêth' as the same thing, contributing to a more textured understanding of how his art responds to the same questions of meaning.

In the next stage of my research, I intend to engage alternative streams in progressive Christian and Jewish thought with the multivocality of Tolkien's own corpus, in order to posit a counter-theodicy to the 'Akallabêth's' metaphysics of blessings and curses. This is, in short, not the only theological game in Arda. For now, I wish to pan the proverbial camera outward to the wider cultural and religious context in which this seminar is taking place. First: 2021 marked the first time in history that fewer than 50 percent of Americans claimed membership in a religious community (Jones 2021). Second: as of writing, Amazon Prime's *The Rings of Power* is well underway in adapting the Second Age of Middle-earth for the silver screen. How the show intends to portray the Downfall of Númenor, with its central motif of a God who condemns an entire continent to controlled demolition, in a television programme aimed at an increasingly nonreligious twenty-first-century audience, remains to be seen. But it points to the continued relevance of the questions Tolkien was asking, and it challenges us as readers and scholars to grapple responsibly with the answers he offers – and pose some questions of our own in turn.

Bibliography

Coogan, Michael, *The Old Testament: A Very Short Introduction*, (Oxford: Oxford University Press, 2008).

Coogan, Michael D. and Cynthia R. Chapman, *A Brief Introduction to the Old Testament: The Hebrew Bible in Its Context*, 3rd ed., (Oxford: Oxford University Press, 2016).

Cooper, Caryn L. and Kevin S. Whetter, 'Hear, O Númenor!: The Covenantal Relationship of the Dúnedain with Ilúvatar', *Journal of Tolkien Research*, 11.2.6 (2020), pp. 1-11.

Fernández Camacho, Pamina, 'Cyclic Cataclysms, Semitic Stereotypes and Religious Reforms: A Classicist's Númenor', in *The Return of the Ring: Proceedings of the Tolkien Society Conference 2012, Vol. 1*, ed. by Lynn Forest-Hill (Edinburgh: Luna Press Publishing, 2016), pp. 191-206.
— 'Elven-Latin and Semitic Adûnaic: Linguistic, Religious, and Political Strife in Tolkien's Island of Númenor', *Journal of Inklings Studies*, 13.1 (2023), pp. 67-86.

Flieger, Verlyn, 'Drowned Lands', in *There Would Always Be a Fairy Tale: More Essays on Tolkien*, (Kent, OH: Kent State University Press, 2017), pp. 213-220.
— *Interrupted Music: The Making of Tolkien's Mythology*, (Kent, OH: Kent State University Press, 2005).

Garth, John, *Tolkien and the Great War: The Threshold of Middle-earth*, (New York: Houghton Mifflin Company, 2003).

Fontenot, Megan N. 'The Art of Eternal Disaster: Tolkien's Apocalypse and the Road to Healing', *Tolkien Studies*, 16 (2019), pp. 91-109.

Heschel, Abraham Joshua. *The Prophets*, (New York: Harper Perennial, 2001).

Jones, Jeffrey M., 'U.S. Church Membership Falls Below Majority for First Time', *Gallup News*, 29 March 2021, <https://news.gallup.com/poll/341963/church-membership-falls-below-majority-first-time.aspx> [accessed 26 June 2023].

Keller, Catherine. *On the Mystery: Discerning Divinity in Process*, (Minneapolis, MN: Fortress Press, 2007).

O'Connor, Kathleen, 'Jeremiah', in *Women's Bible Commentary: Expanded Edition*, ed. by Carol A. Newsom and Sharon H. Ringe (Louisville, KY: Westminster John Knox Press, 1998), pp. 178-186.

Taylor, Charles, *A Secular Age*, (Cambridge, MA: Belknap Press of Harvard University Press, 2007).

Tolkien, J.R.R., *Unfinished Tales of Númenor and Middle-earth*, ed. by Christopher Tolkien (New York: Houghton Mifflin, 1980).
— *The Letters of J.R.R. Tolkien*, ed. by Humphrey Carpenter and Christopher Tolkien (Boston: Houghton Mifflin, 1981).
— *Sauron Defeated*, ed. by Christopher Tolkien (New York: Houghton Mifflin, 1992).
— *The Peoples of Middle-earth*, ed. by Christopher Tolkien (New York: Houghton Mifflin, 1996).
— *The Silmarillion*, 2nd edn, ed. by Christopher Tolkien (New York: Houghton Mifflin, 2001).

Seducer-Destroyer:
Sauron's Femme Fatale Sources and their Role in the Númenor Narrative

Mercury Natis

This paper will look at different biblical femme fatales and how their roles in their own narratives serve as a blueprint for Sauron's role on Númenor. We can then ask the questions: why did Tolkien choose to do this, and how does that influence our reading of the text itself? It is necessary to include a disclaimer here that the following is a critically negative reading of a queer presence in Tolkien's works. Sauron is not a positive character, nor is he positive queer representation. He represents a negative view of what can be understood under a Christian framework as deviant sexuality. This is not the only and therefore definitive queer presence in Tolkien's legendarium. Sauron is just one example of a much more complex conversation on queerness through Tolkien's literary lens.

1 - Tolkien and Femininity: a Theoretical Framework

Before we can discuss how Sauron reflects the tropes of various biblical femme fatales, we must first consider Tolkien's perspectives on women and where we see Tolkien blurring gender boundaries. Within the legendarium, Tolkien's women tend towards moral good. This is not to say that his women are all idealized Madonna figures, but that very few of them are outright evil. Of the three outright evil female characters that Tolkien writes, two of them are relegated to the margins (Queen Berúthiel and Thuringwethil) and the third, Shelob, is a monstrous grotesque creature rather than an embodied woman. None of these women are seductresses or temptresses. What is distinctly lacking in the legendarium is a major evil or wicked feminine presence. While this is a good thing it is unusual, as the move away from wicked women as a major character trope is a very modern development.

Why does Tolkien seem to avoid this? In letter 43 (1941) to his son Michael, Tolkien makes a point to suggest that, as literature has primarily been written by men, women have been significantly generalized as either fair or false, which he calls "on the whole a slander" (*Letters*, Letter 43, 50). Rather, he believed that women are more inclined naturally to loyalty, monogamy, and family life. Men, on the other hand, he is not so quick to forgive. He notes that he thinks men are not instinctively monogamous, and that monogamy in men is a product of faith and ethic (51). Tolkien was well aware of the iconography of the femme fatale, or as Tolkien called it the "false" woman, but perhaps he did not want to write women as such because he did not believe they were an accurate representation of what women were actually like.

Yet the trope is not entirely absent in the legendarium. Tolkien instead applies it to a male-presenting character.[1] In order to understand the transference of gendered tropes across gender boundaries, it is useful to briefly review 'The Feminine Principle in Tolkien' as described by Melanie Rawls

---

1. Giving Sauron's gender and gender presentation proper attention is beyond the scope of this paper. For the purposes of this paper, I will refer to Sauron as male but believe that male-presenting is more accurate given his nature as a Maia and his role as a shape-shifter.

in 1984. While Rawls' paper is greatly in need of an update, it is a very useful tool for understanding the fluidity of gender roles in Tolkien's writing. Rawls identified that Tolkien does not limit traditional gender roles to sex bodies; male characters like Elrond and Faramir can act in feminine ways and female characters like Éowyn can act in masculine ways (1984, 7-10). She identified that in Arda the prime feminine characteristic is understanding and the prime masculine characteristic is power: "feminines give counsel; [...] maculines act" (6). A good feminine is merciful and compassionate, while bad feminines can be anywhere from wholly passive to devouring in their selfishness. In summary, feminines influence the world around them through understanding, through words and emotional attention, whereas masculines influence the world around them through action.

Rawls does refer to Sauron as a "horrible parody of this masculine/feminine interplay" as she identifies that the eye is usually a symbol of femininity but Sauron's eye is outer directed with no interiority or reflection (8-9). Rawls is correct in identifying that Sauron's femininity is a falsehood, a display of understanding that has no real depth, but misses something crucial. In Rawls' own words, "the Feminine Principle shapes individuals. The Masculine Principle shapes events" (10). What Rawls misses is that Sauron does both of these things. In the Second Age, before losing his fair form, Sauron's primary mode of shaping events is *through* shaping individuals and making individuals do the acting in his stead, using people (notably all male characters) as pawns towards their own destruction. Sauron's influence on Ar-Pharazôn is a prime example of this, where he used his feminine characteristics as a tool to shape Númenor's demise.

2 - Sauron on Númenor

Sauron's tenure on Númenor is quite a short episode within the body-text of the legendarium, but it is full of relevant buzzwords and phrases.[2] The devil is truly in the details with regards to Sauron's influence. The story goes as follows: Sauron realized that he could not beat the Númenórians by might, and so he set a trap. Ar-Pharazôn is "filled with the desire of power unbounded" and a desire to compel Sauron as a vassal and servant (*FoN*, 174). Sauron offers no resistance as he was "well skilled to gain what he would by subtlety when force might not avail" (174). He is taken hostage, which is what he wanted, and tells Ar-Pharazôn that "great kings must have their will" (175). We should keep in mind that this dynamic is with us from the onset: the hypermasculine will to dominate and the manipulator, playing at submission, who destroys from a position of perceived lesser power.

Sauron swiftly rose to power on Númenor, seducing the King through the "cunning of his mind and mouth […] for flattery sweet as honey was ever on his tongue" (176).[3] Here we are also reminded that Sauron is beautiful to look upon, and the phrase of power is repeated: "great kings must have their will […] Whatever the king desired he said was his right" (176). Behind locked doors, Sauron convinced Ar-Pharazôn

---

2. This section was accompanied by a slide which listed the various relevant buzzwords not included in the summary. Those include the following: Sauron is described as noble and beautiful, or fair form (*Letters*, Letter 153; *FoN*, 48, 174, 176, 198); Sauron is described as cunning (*Letters*, Letter 131; *FoN*, 171, 176, 221); Sauron "smoothed his tongue" (*FoN*, 174); "temptation" (*Letters*, Letter 131); "the downfall partly the result of an inner weakness of men" (*FoN*, 171).
3. The word "seduce" is not used in *FoN* but can be found in letter 131 (155) and in the Appendices to *The Lord of the Rings* (1084).

that Melkor was the true worshipful God (177). A new religion arose under Sauron, and the Faithful are persecuted and sacrificed at the temple of Melkor under the charge of treason and plotting against their king (180). So it came to be that Sauron "ruled all from behind the throne", and was able to convince Ar-Pharazôn, now "besotted", to launch his attack against the Valar (181). As, after all, "great kings take what is their right" (181).

Ar-Pharazôn is worth analyzing on his own, but that is beyond the scope of this paper. What is important to take away from Ar-Pharazôn for this analysis is that he is hypermasculine. He is the worst embodiment of that active masculinity which Rawls described. He is known to enact violence against women, as he has usurped the throne by marrying Míriel against her will. His position in this narrative is that of power and the desire for more power, which he exerts over others to make them submissive to him. In repeatedly telling Ar-Pharazôn that a king should have what he desires and take what is theirs by right, Sauron encourages this behaviour. He does not do this from the position of an equal but from the position of one subservient. From a position behind the throne that masquerades as supportive, understanding, and most importantly submissive, what Sauron is doing is playing the role of the seducer-destroyer,[4] the femme fatale.

3 - The Victorian Femme Fatale

The femme fatale, as we know her in contemporary Western culture, was born out of a spike in anti-feminist creative output

---

4. This phrasing of femme fatale as seducer-destroyer is taken from Rosina Neginsky's book title, see bibliography.

during the 19th century. Women were gaining more social capital, entering the workforce, and beginning to fight for legal rights and freedoms. It was during this period that artists across mediums were producing the works that Tolkien referred to as slanderous. Women in the arts began to be divided into that fair and false dichotomy: the Marial, virginal angel-of-the-house, or "the dark, dangerous, voluptuous and viraginous woman" (Bach 2010, 211). As explained in great detail by Bram Dijkstra in *Idols of Perversity: Fantasies of Feminine Evil in Fin-de-Siècle Culture* (1988), patriarchal society found a plethora of ways to blame women for all manner of societal ills, as women were an easy scapegoat for the powerlessness of a burgeoning capitalist society (353-66). The seductive woman as the bringer of death was linked to increased prostitution and increased rates of venereal diseases that were ravaging Europe (359). The idea that a woman's desire for riches (itself a product of women being reliant on their husbands for any financial agency) was the root of all progress and all evil was conflated with Eve's desire for the fruit of the tree of knowledge; and so creating a fictitious vision of men's desire to please a beautiful woman as a means towards said progress and evil (366). By 1915, the seductive but deadly woman became a metaphorical symbol for the spirit of war itself (362-3).

A trend had been born and propagated that depicted "women as monsters, predators, seducers and destroyers of men, symbols of evil and perversity […] seductive, evil destroyers, the lustful executioners of men" (Neginsky 2018, 72). But the femme fatale is not exclusively a product of the *fin-de-siècle*. These tropes were only magnified during the *fin-de-siècle*, which then became part of our cultural consciousness through visual and literary rhetoric all the way to today, let's say part of our Cauldron of Story and Tolkien's as well. What these artists did was search far and wide for iconography through which to vent their frustrations, and they did not have to look very far.

Alice Bach's *Women, Seduction, and Betrayal in Biblical Narrative* (2010) is a comprehensive look at biblical narratives in which women exemplify villainy through seduction and betrayal. These biblical stories, Bach explains, draw on the androcentric biblical logic that women, through Eve, "thwarted the divine plan" (2010, 2). The Fall, and in turn original sin, are Eve's fault by this logic and so that stain continues through her line and through the so-called Daughters of Eve. In these biblical narratives, "women offer all sorts of deceitful delicacies to men, who greedily reach out for them no matter what the dangers" (206). The Devil's right hand is so often a woman who exerts power through seductive means. She is Eve, Salome, Lilith, Jezebel, the Whore of Babylon, and Lot's Daughters, to name only a few of the numerous biblical examples. These characters were within easy reach for Victorian artists, as they were for Tolkien, and as they are for us today. As Bach says, "the use of the biblical icon is widespread in our culture […] we are so accustomed to being addressed by these images that we scarcely notice their total impact. Indeed the tropes and figures of the Bible reside in the collective unconscious of Western Culture as well as in the conscious streams of moralizing that drench our popular media" (1).

"Collective unconscious" is a great phrase for Bach to use. It is a Jungian phrase and we know that Tolkien was quite familiar with Jung's work as it influenced his idea of the Cauldron of Story from which we draw our creative influences. We also know that Tolkien was very familiar with biblical narrative. So let us get familiar with some of the biblical femme fatales in our cultural collective unconscious that may have contributed to the blueprint that Tolkien was using in crafting Sauron.

4 - The Whore of Babylon

The Whore of Babylon, a figure in Revelations, ushers in the apocalypse as a metaphor for the false church. She is the bringer of the antiChrist; she gets drunk on the blood of the martyrs; she is so seductive that she is even capable of enamouring saints. The Whore of Babylon may not be a character per se, but she is a useful metaphor. She does, at least in literature, get used quite often not only for what she theologically represents but as a metaphor for the Daughters of Eve as a whole. She often represents an inevitable, apocalypse-bringing feminine figure. We have, in the Whore of Babylon, some similarities with Sauron on Númenor. They are both false prophets, both have the blood of the martyrs on their hands, both have a seductive quality to them and both are the bringer of Doomsday. Not, in Sauron's case, the true Doomsday, but certainly the Númenórian one.

5 - Salome

Salome is not as close a match as the Whore of Babylon in terms of specific details, but Salome represents in our cultural consciousness the apex femme fatale, the ultimate seducer-destroyer, and cannot be completely dismissed from being a potential influence. The bare bones of her story are that Salome dances for King Herod and he is so pleased with what he has seen that he offers her anything she could ask for. She asks for John the Baptist's head in vengeance for his slander against the King and she is given it on a silver platter.

In the Middle Ages, Salome was depicted purely as an evil destroyer, used as a tool to teach John the Baptist's story

(Neginsky 2019, 25). She was not separated from John the Baptist until that 19th-century spike in the iconography of evil women, where Salome became the icon of the femme fatale. She became a symbol of "the dangerous and destructive woman, manipulative through her beauty and through her ability to enslave and destroy men by awakening in them an uncontrollable sexual desire" (Neginsky 2018, 2). As Rosina Neginsky notes in the conclusion of *Salome: The Image of a Woman Who Never Was* (2018), "for society, she became the symbol of the power of destruction for the sake of a new world that she would embody […] [Salome], the whore of Babylon, was depicted as an apocalyptical danger awaiting the world if it gives in to her temptations" (209). Neginsky notes 2,789 works of art and literature made in the 19th century where Salome is the central figure (74).

Yet the question remains: what does Salome have to do with Sauron? The main symbols of Salome's iconography, the beheading and the dance, appear nowhere in Sauron's story. What is significant about Salome is the heavy presence, those 2,789 works of art and literature, that permeated the arts in the 19th century and well into the 20th, and how the story beats of Salome became shorthand for the femme fatale. As noted by Bach, "the figure of Salome […] can be regarded as a place-holder for all the biblical literary figures caught in the tropes of women, women and death" (Bach 2010, 259-60). Tolkien, notably, was not writing allegory. Rather, he took themes out of the Cauldron of Story and used them as a blueprint, and Salome has fed the blueprint in spades. The themes, not the specific iconography, are where Salome may have contributed to Sauron's femme fatale blueprint.

What Salome and Sauron share thematically are the blood of the martyrs on their hands, an emphasis on beauty, and a heavy emphasis on seduction with the victims of that seduction being complicit. In her assessment of Tolkien's use of the word Lust, Emma Hawkins notes that Tolkien seemed to reject the idea that evil just happens to people. Rather than being unsuspecting, innocent victims, evil is made through choices and, in terms of lust, man is complicit in his own ruin (Hawkins 2008, 31). Herod and Ar-Pharazôn, in being subject to their lusts, are seduced but ultimately make the choice to give their seducers exactly what they want. In both cases, the death of the faithful is a benefit to the King as a means of removing their biggest detractors.

As Salome is, in terms of our cultural collective unconscious and the Cauldron of Story, our apex femme fatale, then her iconography of seducing the King and of the gleeful murdering of saints cannot be entirely ignored even if the specific details do not match. This results in fanart like Dorothea Sophia's *Tar-Mairon*, where the tray and the knife create a logical association.[5]

6 - Jezebel

Jezebel is our closest iconographical match. Jezebel was the queen married to King Ahab of Israel. A worshipper of Baal, Jezebel used her power and influence to turn Israel towards the cult of Baal and had followers of Yahweh brutally murdered. She also has an innocent man murdered for blasphemy against Baal and treason against the King. While there is no mention of sexuality in Jezebel's narrative, and biblically speaking she does not use her beauty and sexuality to get what she wants,

---

5. A work of fanart by Dorothea Sophia (also known as busymagpie), of Sauron holding a tray in one hand, with a bloody knife in the other: https://www.deviantart.com/dorotheasophia/art/Tar-Mairon-792866560.

only her power as Queen, beauty and vanity have become associated with her over time due to her painting her face before her death (Deez 2019). With that association, when thrown into the Cauldron of femme fatale Story, comes the idea that has stayed with Jezebel as a character: that of the false prophet who manipulates through seduction to lead the faithful to idolatry.

We can see many parallels between Jezebel and Sauron. Both are false prophets who lead chosen people astray and into idolatry, both sacrifice the faithful to their Gods, and both masquerade their murders as being punishments for blasphemy and treason. They are both also the power behind the throne and are both associated with beauty.

These three characters are not the be-all end-all of associations that can be made between Sauron and femme fatales. If I were to look beyond the Bible, I could, for example, immediately draw parallels to Lady Macbeth. What these three examples bring are three major points of comparison within Tolkien's direct frame of reference. All three have the blood of the martyrs on their hands. Jezebel and the Whore of Babylon are false prophets, and Salome is the seducer. Sauron is not an allegorical but an amalgamation. This blueprint comes directly from female characters and is put onto this male character. It is the blueprint of the *Ishah Zarah*.

7 - The *Ishah Zarah*

What follows is an analysis of biblical scripture as a work of literature with specific iconography that is a primary influence on Tolkien's writing, rather than a discussion of deeper theological meaning. For ease, I am going to be quoting primarily from the King James translation, but I will include the most important line in four translations with which Tolkien would also have been familiar.[6] The *Ishah Zarah* is translated differently across these editions. She is the Strange Woman, the harlot, the false woman, the whore, the adulteress.[7] As all of these translations mean different things, I will use *Ishah Zarah* for this analysis.

In Proverbs 5:3-23, we can see strong parallels with Sauron and Ar-Pharazôn's Númenor story. In these lines, the reader is told not to give in to the temptation of the sinful other, who seduces with honeyed words, and to do so will lead to death and hell. This full section of Proverbs requires substantial, extensive analysis for a deeper comparison to be made, which is beyond the scope of this paper. This paper will focus solely on lines 3-5, and then lines 22-23.

King James	3. For **the lips of a strange woman drop as an honeycomb**, and her mouth is smoother than oil;
	4. But her end is bitter as wormwood, sharp as a two-edged sword.
	5. Her feet go down to death; her steps take hold in hell.
	22. His own iniquities shall take the wicked himself, and he shall be holden with the chords of his sins.

---

6. These four translations have been selected based on advice from Tolkien scholars more involved in Tolkien's theological history than myself.

7. It is important to note that, while the best contemporary translation from Hebrew of "zarah" is "foreign", we are looking at a Christian theological perspective which has repeatedly translated the word differently for their own purposes, and thus influenced interpretation.

King James	23. **He shall die without instruction; and the greatness of his folly he shall go astray.**[8]

Douay-Rheims	3. For **the lips of a harlot are like a honeycomb dropping**, and her throat is smoother than oil.
Wycliffe	3. Give thou not attention to **the falseness of a woman; for the lips of an whore be an honeycomb dropping**, and her throat is clearer than oil;
New Jerusalem	3. **For the lips of the adulteress drip with honey**, her palate is more unctuous than oil;

There are two major parallels here with the story of Sauron on Númenor. The first is the use of the word honeycomb or honey. All four translations describe her words as like honey that drops from her lips. Honey is also found in the Latin Vulgate and in the Greek. This is the exact language that Tolkien uses to describe Sauron, except he changes lips to tongue: "yet **such was the cunning of his mind and mouth**, and the strength of his hidden will, that ere three years had passed he had become closest to the secret counsels of the King; for flattery sweet as honey was ever on his tongue" (*FoN*, 176). Given all of the parallels between the *Ishah Zarah*, the biblical femme fatale, and Sauron, and given Tolkien's great familiarity with scripture, I find it extremely likely that this phrasing is intentional. We can also note that the Wycliffe translation refers to the *Ishah Zarah* as a "false woman", which was Tolkien's own phrasing

---

[8]. In some other translations, the word "deceived" is used instead of "astray".

as well in regards the literary femme fatale.

This parallel is supported by the second important part of this quoted section, lines 22 and 23. As we know, Tolkien rejected the idea that evil just happens to people; Ar-Pharazôn is a key example of evil that is chosen and that one does to himself. This section of Proverbs puts the blame for wickedness on the man who goes astray by his own folly. Ar-Pharazôn serves as an example for the warning that this section of Proverbs provides.

8 - Sauron's Femme Fatale Presence as a Methodology of Power

What we are seeing in Sauron and Ar-Pharazôn's relationship is a complex power dynamic that is usually presented in gendered terms. Women, in our patriarchal society, have been for most of history in a position of disadvantage in terms of power. The femme fatale is in many ways a representation of the fear that women may use their disadvantaged position to gain power, and so take that power away from men. It is, as Maria Alberto notes in her paper on Tolkien's use of seduction in his legendarium, that "ultimately, the nature of seduction is deceit and manipulation; the purpose of seduction is the attempted increase of power" (Alberto 2017, 65). This is the crux of the spike of the femme fatale in 19th-century art and literature that pours gallons of this trope into the Cauldron of Story. The way that Sauron enacts his power over Ar-Pharazôn is through the means of the femme fatale. He manipulates Ar-Pharazôn into taking him to Númenor, where he subjugates and submits himself to Ar-Pharazôn's voracious need for hyper-masculine dominance. Through honeyed words and a beautiful face, through the means of seduction available to the femme fatale, Sauron takes the position of power through the guise of being behind the throne, not on it.

In 'The Feminine Principle in Tolkien', Rawls notes that "where masculine and feminine are in harmony there is good, but evil is a result of insufficiency or disharmony of one or the other" (1984, 5). In this case, evil is found in a cacophonous disharmony of the masculine and the feminine where they are both fighting for control rather than actually working together. As per Rawls' observation that Sauron's eye is outward-focused, Sauron's femininity is an illusion. Sauron's feminine principle influences Ar-Pharazôn's hand to move events, but Sauron is in control and is really the one who is powerful. As such, Ar-Pharazôn goes so far astray and is so thoroughly deceived that he follows the *Ishah Zarah* down to hell. It is no mistake that Tolkien uses the word "lust" as a metaphor for the will to power, this bodily drive to dominate.[9]

Tolkien chose to use this trope of the *Ishah Zarah*, the femme fatale, but as he did not want to apply it to women, so he chose to apply it to a male character. This is fundamentally a queering action. This makes Sauron a queer character by all definitions of the word "queer", within a very well-established tradition of the queer-coded villain.[10] Sauron is presented on Númenor as a feminine character with feminine traits, and the villain of a seduction piece is now a man who seduces other men.

Due to the constraints of this paper, I cannot delve into the moralistic connotations and consequences of this decision, though they are worth addressing in future iterations of this

---

9. I aim to elaborate on this in a future paper, as an addition to Emma Hawkins' assessment of Tolkien's use of the word "lust".

10. I also aim to elaborate on this in a future paper, but am unable to do so here due to the constraints of this paper. This has been argued in brief by Danna Petersen-Deeprose in their entry for the Tolkien Society Seminar 2021 proceedings *Tolkien and Diversity* (2023).

research. I do not think this is the definitive example of Tolkien's relationship with queerness, but it certainly is a relationship to a very specific version of queerness, in which Sauron embodies a version of so-called deviant sexuality at its very worst. While it has been well argued by Maria Alberto and Emma Hawkins that Tolkien uses the words "seduction" and "lust" metaphorically or archaically, that does not change the inherently sexual nature of this particular dynamic, of which he was well aware. The proof is in the iconography. In Tolkien's own words, "the dislocation of the sex-instinct is one of the chief symptoms of the Fall" (*Letters*, Letter 43, 48); "the devil is endlessly ingenious, and sex is his favourite subject" (48). It is no mistake that Tolkien describes Ar-Pharazôn as "besotted" by Sauron, a word that means to be foolishly infatuated.

It is very common for critics against queer readings of Tolkien's work to comment that Tolkien was an author with Victorian sensibilities and therefore would not have understood these concepts. Putting aside the fact that he wasn't a Victorian author but a 20th-century author with an Edwardian youth, these patterns of representation are distinctly Victorian. The blueprint for the seductive harlot, the false prophet bathed in the blood of the martyrs who passively rather than actively manipulates the men around them is firmly Victorian, as part of what Bram Dijkstra refers to as the "veritable iconography of misogyny" present in *fin-de-siècle* art (1988, viii). That Tolkien did not want to write about evil women and so transcribed this blueprint onto a male presenting character is in itself a queerness.

Bibliography

Alberto, Maria, '"It Had Been His Virtue, And Therefore Also The Cause Of His Fall": Seduction As A Mythopoeic Accounting For Evil In Tolkien's Work', *Mythlore*, 35.2 (2017).

Anon., 'Proverbs 5:3-23' in *Douay-Rheims 1899 American Edition*, BibleGateway.com, <https://www.biblegateway.com/passage/?search=Proverbs+5%3A3-23&version=DRA> [accessed 4 August 2023].

Anon., 'Proverbs 5:3-23' in *New King James Version*, BibleGateway.com, <https://www.biblegateway.com/passage/?search=Proverbs+5%3A3-23&version=NKJV> [accessed 4 August 2023].

Anon., 'Proverbs 5:3-23' in *Wycliffe Bible*, BibleGateway.com, <https://www.biblegateway.com/passage/?search=Proverbs+5%3A3-23&version=WYC> [accessed 4 August 2023].

Anon. 'Proverbs 5' in *New Jerusalem Bible*, Bíblia Católica Online, <http://www.bibliacatolica.com.br/> [accessed 4 August 2023]

Bach, Alice, *Women, Seduction, and Betrayal in Biblical Narrative*, (Cambridge: Cambridge University Press, 2010).

Deez, Genie, *Problems with Images of Jezebel*, Genie Deez ENT LTD, 2019 <http://www.geniedeez.tv/blog/2019/4/17/problems-with-images-of-jezebel> [accessed 21 June 2023].

Dijkstra, Bram, *Idols of Perversity: Fantasies of Feminine Evil in Fin-de-Siècle Culture*, revised ed., (New York: Oxford University Press, 1988).

Hawkins, Emma B., 'Tolkien's Linguistic Application of the Seventh Deadly Sin: Lust', *Mythlore*, 26.3 (2008), pp. 29–40.

Neginsky, Rosina, *Salome: The Image of a Woman Who Never Was; Nymph, Seducer, Destroyer,* (Newcastle-upon-Tyne: Cambridge Scholars Publishing, 2018).

Petersen-Deeprose, Danna, '"Something Mighty Queer": Destabilizing Cishetero Amatonormativity in the Works of Tolkien', in Tolkien and

Diversity, ed. by Will Sherwood, (Luna Press Publishing, 2023), pp. 119–139.

Rawls, Melanie, 'The Feminine Principle in Tolkien', *Mythlore*, 10.4 (1984), pp. 5–13.

Tolkien, J.R.R., *The Fall of Númenor and Other Tales from the Second Age of Middle-earth*, ed. by Brian Sibley, (London: HarperCollins, 2022).
— *The Letters of J.R.R. Tolkien*, ed. by Humphrey Carpenter with the assistance of Christopher Tolkien (London: HarperCollins, 2006).
— *The Return of the King*, (London: HarperCollins, 2020).
— *The Silmarillion*, ed. by Christopher Tolkien, (Boston: Houghton Mifflin, 2001).

Elmar, the Experience of Captured Women, and Empires in Decline

Clare Moore

In the year 2023, a comparison between Tolkien and Anglo-Saxonism is the furthest thing from revolutionary. Connections to Anglo-Saxon history, language, and poetry with Tolkien's fiction, personal interests, and professional career are abundant in Tolkien scholarship – established most notably by Tom Shippey (*The Road to Middle-earth*, 2003), Michael Drout ('A Mythology for Anglo-Saxon England', 2004), and Thomas Honegger ('The Rohirrim: "Anglo-Saxons on Horseback"?', 2011). The connection offered in this paper is off this well-worn path and a bit more speculative, but it will still offer insight into Tolkien's fiction and creative process. By comparing the Second Age story of Elmar, an enslaved Númenórean woman, with the character Flavia from Rosemary Sutcliff's 1959 historical fiction novel *The Lantern Bearers*, this paper suggests that in writing Elmar's story Tolkien is imagining the female experience of the Saxon invasion of England in the fifth century following the withdrawal of the Roman Empire from Britain. In doing so, Tolkien offers a creative solution to a perpetual lacuna in the historical record from this time period: an account of the life of an ordinary woman.

Tolkien describes Anglo-Saxon history as "a period mostly filled with most intriguing Question Marks" (*Letters*, Letter 95, 108), and this is especially true of the beginning of this time period. The fifth century saw the removal of the Roman military from Britain, precipitating the collapse of the region's economy and cities. Into this depressed Britain, came the Saxons. The coming of the Saxons to Britain was long understood as an invasion, a perception based primarily on the literary-historical record of Bede's *Ecclesiastical History of the English People* (731 C.E.), Gildas' *On the Ruin of Britain* (sixth century), and the *Anglo-Saxon Chronicle* (ninth century). However, the understanding of this history has shifted in recent decades. Modern archeological and DNA research reveals that Angles, Saxons, Jutes, and other people groups migrated to Britain from mainland Europe, often in peaceful family units that integrated over time with existing Celtic and Romano-British communities. Contemporary researchers have also abandoned the term 'Anglo-Saxon' since it is ahistorical, generalized, and loaded with racist and nationalist connotations. Instead, researchers utilize more specific and descriptive terminology to reference people groups and concepts from this time period, such as 'Angles' or 'Old English'. This paper will discuss the specific people group who migrated to Britain in the largest numbers and thus had the largest impact on fictional imaginings of Britain's fifth century history: the Saxons. It will, however, reference the coming of the Saxons to Britain as an invasion, reflecting the cultural conception of this history during Tolkien's lifetime. It is a Saxon invasion, not migration, that is reflected in the text 'Tal-Elmar'.

'Tal-Elmar' is one of Tolkien's more obscure writings concerning the Second Age. Found in *The Peoples of Middle-earth* (2002), the final volume of *The Histories of Middle-earth*, and written in the 1950s, this short text recounts the story of Tal-Elmar, the grandson of Elmar, a Númenórean woman who lived in a colonial settlement in Middle-earth before being captured by Buldar, one of the Wild Men of the Hills of Agar, during the wars between the Wild Men and Númenóreans. Buldar enslaves Elmar and marries her. They have multiple children, and Elmar spends the rest of her life in the Hills of Agar. After a brief account of Elmar's life, the text moves on to tell the story of her grandson, which Tolkien never finished.

Sutcliff, a noted children's historical fiction writer of the 20th century, published her novel *The Lantern Bearers* in 1959. *The Lantern Bearers* is the third book of a series known as *The Dolphin Cycle*. The first of these books is *The Eagle of the Ninth* (1954), which was adapted into an entertaining film of questionable quality starring Channing Tatum, Jamie Bell, and Mark Strong in 2011. *The Lantern Bearers* follows the story of Aquila, a Romano-British soldier who decides to remain in Britain when the Roman military leaves. Almost immediately, a Saxon raiding party attacks his home, kills his father, abducts his sister Flavia, and leaves him for dead. He is 'rescued' by a Jute raiding party, enslaved to one of their elders, and brought to a Saxon settlement where he is unexpectedly reunited with his sister, whom he learns is married to the nephew of the Saxon who murdered their father and has born that man a son. Flavia helps Aquila escape but refuses to leave with him.

Sutcliff's book takes place in fifth century Britain and documents the story of a young Romano-British woman captured by Saxons and forced into marriage, motherhood, and a foreign culture. Flavia's fictional story conveys an experience almost always lost to the archeological, historical, and literary record: the female experience of violence during a momentous historical transition, such as the collapse of an empire. Tolkien's tale takes place in the fictional Middle-earth, but the parallels between Elmar and Flavia's narratives suggest that Tolkien drew upon his understanding of this real-world history in shaping Elmar's story. Or, at the very least, these parallels offer insight into how we can interpret Elmar's story and find meaning within her very brief text because her narrative also documents the female experience of an empire's decline, of capture and enslavement, of forced marriage and motherhood, of the conflicts of identity and culture, and of the reality of lives lived in the margins of great historical moments.

Elmar's narrative shares several key elements with Flavia's that bring Elmar's story into alignment with a narrative of the female experience of the Saxon invasion. First, Númenor resembles the Roman Empire, casting the Númenórean settlers of Middle-earth as the Romano-British people of fifth century England, while the Wild Men resemble the Saxon invaders. These similarities manifest physically, linguistically, and culturally. Second, Elmar and Flavia's stories share the same plot progression. They are captured during a violent attack, forced to marry one of their attackers, have children with these men, and spend the rest of their lives living in this forced, foreign community. Thirdly, through their lived experience of this distinctly female ordeal, both Elmar and Flavia demonstrate the impact of empires and their decline on the lives of those often marginalized by history.

The similarities between the Númenóreans and Romans and the Wild Men and Saxons are found in the juxtaposition between the two opposing races. Philosopher Charles W. Mills, whose essay 'The Wretched of Middle-earth: An Orkish Manifesto' was written in the 1980s but published posthumously in 2022 (Jeffers and Gray 2022, 2), proposes that Tolkien constructs his races in terms of aesthetics (including physical appearance, morality, and social order), language, and culture (Mills 2022, 8). Along these lines, Tal-Elmar's Númenórean genetic inheritance from his grandmother includes being tall, white, and respectful of other people (*Peoples*, 423). Though he speaks the language of the Wild Men, he makes it lovelier to hear (423), and when he encounters sailors from Númenor on the shore near his home, he "feels the language to be *known* and only thinly veiled from him" (435). Overall, Tolkien describes Tal-Elmar as one of an "alien people" living among an "ignoble people" (423). Tal-Elmar's racial superiority, demonstrated through his fair – meaning both beautiful and white – appearance, his respectful morality, his perception of language, and his cultural identity as an "alien" living among "ignoble people", derives from his Númenórean grandmother. It is Elmar who is beautiful and white, speaks an aesthetic language, and hails from a superior culture. This directly contrasts Tolkien's construction of the Wild Men, who are "broad, swarthy, short, tough, harsh-tongued, heavy-handed, and quick to violence" (423). In one sentence, Tolkien confirms the aesthetic, linguistic, and cultural inferiority of the Wild Men in opposition to the Númenóreans.

As a Romano-British woman, Flavia's aesthetics are also elevated over that of the opposing race: the Saxons. Flavia has black hair, "harsh as a stallion's mane, and so full of life that she could comb sparks out of it" (Sutcliff 1959, 3), and though her dark hair may seem to contrast Elmar's whiteness, Flavia's beauty is still presented as "fair", meaning beautiful – much like Tolkien presents Lúthien as fair but dark-haired – and Flavia is still described as white (78). The aesthetics of the Saxons directly contrast that of Flavia and Aquila. Sutcliff describes the Saxons as yellow-haired (28), but also as big, broad-faced, and other terms reminiscent of Tolkien's "swarthy" Wild Men (69). Compared to Flavia and Aquila's Latin, the Saxon language is guttural (29), and – of course – it is the violent Saxons who attack a peaceful Romano-British farm. Therefore, racial superiority links the Númenóreans and the Romano-British people, and racial inferiority links the barbaric and violent Wild Men and Saxons.

Within the conflicts between these opposing races, Elmar and Flavia experience a similar progression of events. First, they are captured and abducted from their homes. From the war with the Númenóreans, Buldar, Tal-Elmar's grandfather, brings back "as booty" "a wound, and a sword, and a woman", the woman being Elmar (*Peoples*, 424). When Saxons attack Aquila's family's farm, Flavia is carried off, shrieking her brother's name and "struggling like a wildcat, over the shoulder of a laughing, fair-haired giant" (Sutcliff 1959, 28). Once captured, both Elmar and Flavia are forced to marry their abductors. Tolkien writes that Elmar was "fortunate; for the fate of the captives was short and cruel, but Buldar took her as his wife. For she was beautiful" (*Peoples*, 424). In the Saxon settlement, Aquila recognizes Flavia because she wears their father's ring (Sutcliff 1959, 65), which she later tells him she received as a bride price from the Saxon who carried her off (68).

In both of these situations, it is important to recognize that marriage does not nullify the violence of Elmar or Flavia's experience. Elmar identifies herself as a captive (*Peoples*, 425), but her condition should be defined as enslavement. Philosopher Michael Rota summarizes two standards for identifying an enslaved person. First, that they are controlled to a level equivalent to that of an object and, second, they are exploited for the advantage of the controlling group or individual (Rota 2020, 560). Buldar's control of Elmar is clear, since he tells her it is vain to try to escape from him (*Peoples*, 425), and Rota notes that "the exploitation condition is met in all cases of forced marriage, as non-consensual sex always involves the intention to use a person as a means to the attainment of an (apparent) good that is not shared by both parties" (2020,

561). Likewise, Flavia is abducted by force, and the necessity of an escape plan implies that she is not free to leave the Saxon settlement. She also tells Aquila that she belongs to her husband (Sutcliff 1959, 79), demonstrating his control of her to the level of objectification. Like Elmar, Flavia is also exploited for sex and reproduction. Without control of their own bodies, then, both women's sexual encounters should be understood as rape. Thus, while we can view these relationships as marriages, we must simultaneously interpret them as enslavement and sexual violence.

As a result of these marriages, Elmar and Flavia both have children. Elmar bears Buldar multiple children, to whom "she spoke much when none were by, and she sang to them many songs in a strange fair tongue; but they heeded her not, or soon forgot. Save only Hazad, the youngest", who is Tal-Elmar's father (*Peoples*, 425). When Aquila meets Flavia again, she has a small child playing at her feet, "a man-child of about a year old" (Sutcliff 1959, 65). When Aquila asks Flavia what happened to her, she gestures to the child "as though that answered the whole question" (66).

Forced into these lives, into marriage and motherhood, both Elmar and Flavia remain in these foreign communities the rest of their days. Elmar tells Buldar,

> If here I must dwell, then dwell I must, as one whose body is in this place at thy will, but my thought far elsewhere. And this vengeance I shall have, that while my body is kept here in exile, the lot of all this folk shall worsen, and thine most; but when my body goes to the alien earth, and my thought is free of it, then in thy kin one shall arise who is mine alone. And with his arising shall come the end of thy people and the downfall of your king. (*Peoples*, 425)

After this speech, Elmar is "a woman of few words while her life lasted" (425).

In the Saxon settlement, Flavia helps Aquila escape and he asks her to come with him. She tells him she cannot leave her child, and he tells her to bring her son as well. Still, Flavia will not leave because she cannot leave her husband either (Sutcliff 1959, 78). When Aquila asks if this is love or hate, Flavia responds, "I do not know. Something of both maybe; but it doesn't make any difference. I belong to him" (79). When they part for the last time, she tells him, "remember me sometimes—even though it hurts to remember" (79). Years later, Aquila meets Flavia's son and learns that she is still alive and living in the Saxon community (209).

Both Elmar and Flavia's stories of loss and suffering are shaped by the dynamics of empire. Elmar lives in Middle-earth because of Númenor's colonial expansion. This expansion directly causes the wars with the Wild Men, which results in Elmar's capture and enslavement. Flavia and her family are left vulnerable to Saxon invaders when the Roman Empire recalls its military from Britain. At first sight, these situations seem the opposite of each other. Númenor is expanding and Rome is retracting. But both of these empires can be viewed as in decline. When Rome recalled its military from Britain at the beginning of the fifth century in order to reinforce its defenses closer to home, the empire was already "only a distant relative" of the Rome that had conquered and colonized Britain (Fleming 2010, 1). By this time, the Roman empire had split in two and was besieged by Germanic tribes. Despite gathering its military forces in mainland Europe, Rome would be sacked by the Visigoths in 410 C.E., and the Roman Empire would collapse completely before the end of the century.

Númenor is an expanding colonial empire during Elmar's

lifetime, but this rise in power occurs simultaneously with its moral decline. Indeed, Númenor's rise to power is inextricably linked with its moral decline, exemplified by its colonial expansion, worship of Morgoth, and forced royal marriages. What begins as unfair taxation – happy Fourth of July to the United States – quickly turns into colonial settlement. Buldar tells Elmar that her people are thieves, "for our lands are ours from of old, which they would wrest from us with their bitter blades. White skins and bright eyes are no warrant for such deeds" (*Peoples*, 425). When Tal-Elmar finally meets the Númenórean sailors who land on the shore, they tell him, "your time of dwelling in these hills is come to an end. Here the men of the West have resolved to make their homes, and the folk of the dark must depart – or be slain" (437). In this scene, the Númenóreans explicitly state their intentions to take the land for themselves and threaten genocide to anyone who stands in their way.

Númenor's colonial expansion happens simultaneously with its shift from following Ilúvatar to a desire for immortality and ultimately following Sauron and the cult he establishes on the island. Buldar tells his son Tal-Elmar that Númenóreans have not come to the Hills of Agar since his father Buldar's days, when they came "only to raid and catch men and depart" (427). If they return to the shores of Middle-earth, it is to "bear away evil booty, captives packed like beasts, the fairest women and children, or young men unblemished […] Some say that they are eaten for meat; and others that they are slain in torment on the black stones in the worship of the Dark" (427). Buldar's rumors prove to be true, as, under Sauron's influence, Númenóreans worship Morgoth, first secretly and then openly through practices that include human sacrifice (*FoN*, 177-80).

Númenor's moral decline during this time is also marked

by two forced royal marriages: Ar-Gimilzôr's marriage to Inzilbêth (*FoN*, 165) and Ar-Pharazôn's marriage to Tar-Míriel (168). Ar-Gimilzôr is described as "the greatest enemy of the Faithful that had yet arisen. In his day the White Tree was untended and began to decline; and he forbade utterly the use of the Elven-tongues, and punished those that welcomed the ships of Eressëa […] He revered nothing, and went never to the Hallow of Eru" (164), while Ar-Pharazôn is well known as the king who sails to Aman under the influence of Sauron, causing the Valar to ask Eru to sink the island of Númenor (186-9). Despite Númenor's rising political and economic power, then, it is clearly an empire in moral decline, as demonstrated by its violent colonial expansion, violent religious practices, and violent royal marriages. Númenor's colonial expansion, religious practices, and royal marriages only further align it with the Roman Empire.

The stories of Elmar and Flavia are deeply moving. Tolkien and Sutcliff keenly portray the violence, pain, and loss these two women experience as the result of the broader conflicts of empires. By telling these stories, both Tolkien and Sutcliff fill a gap in the historical record, offering a personal and sympathetic account of a female experience of the historic fifth century. Through this lens, it is possible to see Tolkien as writing historical fanfiction in order to explore one of the many question marks left by history.

Bibliography

Drout, Michael D.C., 'A Mythology for Anglo-Saxon England', in *Tolkien and the Invention of Myth: A Reader*, ed. by Jane Chance (University Press of Kentucky, 2004), pp. 229-247.

Fleming, Robin, *Britain after Rome: The Fall and Rise, 400-1070*, (Allen Lane, 2010).

Honegger, Thomas, 'The Rohirrim: "Anglo-Saxons on Horseback"? An inquiry into Tolkien's use of sources', in *Tolkien and the Study of His Sources: Critical Essays*, ed. by Jason Fisher (MacFarland, 2011), pp. 116-132.

Jeffers, Chike and David Miguel Gray, 'Introduction to Charles Mills's "The Wretched of Middle-earth: An Orkish Manifesto"', *The Southern Journal of Philosophy*, 60.1 (2022), pp. 102-104.

Mills, Charles W., 'The Wretched of Middle-earth: An Orkish Manifesto', *The Southern Journal of Philosophy*, 60.1 (2022), pp. 105-135.

Rota, Michael, 'On the Definition of Slavery', *Theoria*, 86 (2020), pp. 543-564.

Shippey, Tom, *The Road to Middle-earth*, (Houghton Mifflin Company, 2003).

Sutcliff, Rosemary, *The Lantern Bearers*, (Farrar Straus Giroux, 1959).

Tolkien, J.R.R., *The Letters of J.R.R. Tolkien*, ed. by Humphrey Carpenter with the assistance of Christopher Tolkien (Houghton Mifflin Company, 2000).
— *The Peoples of Middle-earth*, ed. by Christopher Tolkien (Harper Collins, 2015).

— *The Fall of Númenor*, ed. by Brian Sibley (Harper Collins, 2022)

About the contributors

Putri Prihatini is the author of *The Lore Master: Blog Tolkien Indonesia*. An Indonesian of Javanese descent and a folklore enthusiast, she is interested in exploring themes and elements behind Tolkien's works and their parallels with her cultural background, noting how reading Tolkien has motivated her to learn more about her cultural traditions. Her blog post 'The Names of Túrin Turambar and Spiritual Burden Concept in Javanese Naming Philosophy' was presented at *Tolkien the Pagan* (2018) and 'Greed and Blood: Powerful Objects in *The Silmarillion* and Javanese *Book of Monarchs*' was nominated for Best Article in Tolkien Society Awards 2021.

Irina Metzler is a former lecturer in medieval history with a PhD in the history of medicine. She has a long-standing interest in Tolkien's work through her personal journey from fandom to scholarly engagement, with a number of Oxonmoot and seminar talks; she had a previous Tolkien Seminar paper on Tolkien and disability published in the Peter Roe series.

S.R. Westvik is an independent scholar focusing on Second Age subjects including Númenor and the character Elendil, examined particularly through the lenses of trauma, war history, and imperialism. Awarded an MA in International War Studies from University College Dublin and the University of Potsdam in 2023 with a focus on the Pacific Theatre of the Second World War, they have previously spoken at *Tolkien 2019*, *Oxonmoot* (2021), and the Leeds International Medieval Congress (2023). They co-host the *Tolkien Experience Podcast* and regularly contribute to Tolkien-related events and fora, both social and academic.

Sara Brown is Director of the Graduate Program and Chair of the Language and Literature Faculty at Signum University, USA, where she has taught on courses with Corey Olsen, Verlyn Flieger, Dimitra Fimi, Robin Reid, Doug Anderson, Amy Sturgis, and John Garth. Sara currently serves on the editorial board of *Mallorn*, the academic journal of the Tolkien Society, and is co-presenter on podcasts such as *The Tolkien Experience*, *The Rings of Power Wrap-Up*, *Rings and Rituals* and *The Prancing Pony*. She won the Tolkien Society Award for Best Article in both 2023 and 2024, and is currently working on a book, *Transgressive Tolkien*, with Christopher Vaccaro.

Journee Cotton is an Assistant Professor of English at New Mexico Military Institute. She is a sponsor for the institute's English Club "Post Script". She received bachelor degrees from Lubbock Christian University in English with an emphasis in Literature and Humanities with an emphasis in Law and a master's degree in English Literature specialising in the Victorian and Romantic periods at the University of Bristol, and her PhD from the University of Exeter studying English. She is co-running a Tolkien Society seminar "Arda's Entangled Bodies and Environments". She is interested in bioethics, ecology, Victorian literature, and the representation of the body in literature.

Muhammed Alpaslan Tandırcı, born in Eskişehir, Turkey, in 1996, currently resides in Istanbul. He received his master's degree in Political Science and Public Administration from Bursa Uludağ University in 2022, with a thesis entitled

"Eco-Critical Analysis of Tolkien Legendarium from an Environmental History Perspective." He is presently pursuing his PhD in Political Science and Public Administration at Kırıkkale University. In 2024, he served as both editor-in-chief and contributor to *The Tolkien Universe – Essays on J.R.R. Tolkien and Middle-earth*, the first comprehensive volume on Tolkien Studies published in Turkey. He continues his academic career as a research assistant, with a particular focus on political theory, environmental thought, and literary studies.

Erik Jampa Andersson is the author of *Unseen Beings: How We Forgot the World is More than Human* (Hay House: May 2023) and a postgraduate student at Goldsmiths, University of London, where he specialises in Environmental History and the History of Medicine. His thesis focuses on Tibetan nature spirit paradigms at the intersection of ecology, mythology, religion, and health. Erik is a graduate of the Shang Shung Institute School of Tibetan Medicine, and teaches globally on Tibetan and Buddhist studies. He has been an avid reader of Tolkien's works for 25 years.

Kristine Larsen has been an astronomy professor at Central Connecticut State University since 1989. Her teaching and research focus on the intersections between science and society, including science and popular culture (especially science in the works of J.R.R. Tolkien) and the history of science. She is the author of the books *Stephen Hawking: A Biography, Cosmology 101, The Women Who Popularized Geology in the 19th Century, Particle Panic!, Science, Technology and Magic in The Witcher* (2023), and *The Sun We Share* (2024).

The **Rev. Tom Emanuel** is a minister and theologian in the United Church of Christ and a doctoral researcher with the Centre for Fantasy and the Fantastic at the University of Glasgow. His work exploring Tolkien, religion, and the post-Christian spiritual landscape of the twenty-first century has appeared in the Journal of *Tolkien Research, Mallorn, Mythlore*, and *Tolkien Studies*, among other venues. Tom currently lives and works in Scotland but will soon be rejoining his family in the United States.

Mercury Natis is a PhD candidate in English Literature and History at the University of Glasgow, researching the queer historical contexts in which Tolkien lived and their influence on his works. They hold an MA in Museum Education and a BA in Art History, with coursework in Tolkien Studies through Signum University. Their work focuses on queer ambiguity in the fantastic prior to the 1960s, with special interests in camp performativity and the First World War cultural ethos. They have presented on similar topics at *Oxonmoot*, *Glasgow International Fantasy Conversations* and the Mythopoeic Society's *Online Midyear Seminar*.

Clare Moore is a Ph.D. student at the University of Glasgow, researching disability in Tolkien's legendarium. She holds an M.F.A. in Creative Writing and a B.A. in Politics, Philosophy, and Economics. Her research focuses on disability, gender, and race in the works of J.R.R. Tolkien, and her work has appeared in *Mallorn*, *Journal of Tolkien Research*, and *Mythlore*. Her essay 'A Song of Greater Power: Tolkien's Construction of Lúthien Tinúviel' won the 2022 Tolkien Society Award for Best Article.

www.ingramcontent.com/pod-product-compliance
Lightning Source LLC
Chambersburg PA
CBHW071200070526
44584CB00019B/2864